This book belongs to:

Dedication

This vision board notebook is dedicated to anyone who has a dream and wants to make it a reality.

May all your visions became true!

How To Use This Vision Board Book

This vision board notebook is dedicated to anyone who has a dream and wants to make it a reality.

This useful vision board journal is a must-have for anyone that loves to dream! You will love this easy to use journal to track and record all your vision board activities.

Each interior page includes space to record & track the following:
Goals - Write down the goals you currently have.
Bucket List - Use this space to list out your creative travel plans.
Inspirational Quotes - Stay on task using the space to write out favorite sayings.
Money - Record and Track your money goals.
Relationships - Use this heart space to list out dreams and desires.
Wellbeing - Project plan your goals for healthy living.
Career - Use this space to list out job and education goals.
If you are new to the world of vision board making or have been at it for a while, this vision board notebook is a must have! Can make a great useful gift for anyone that loves to plan for the future!

Have Fun!

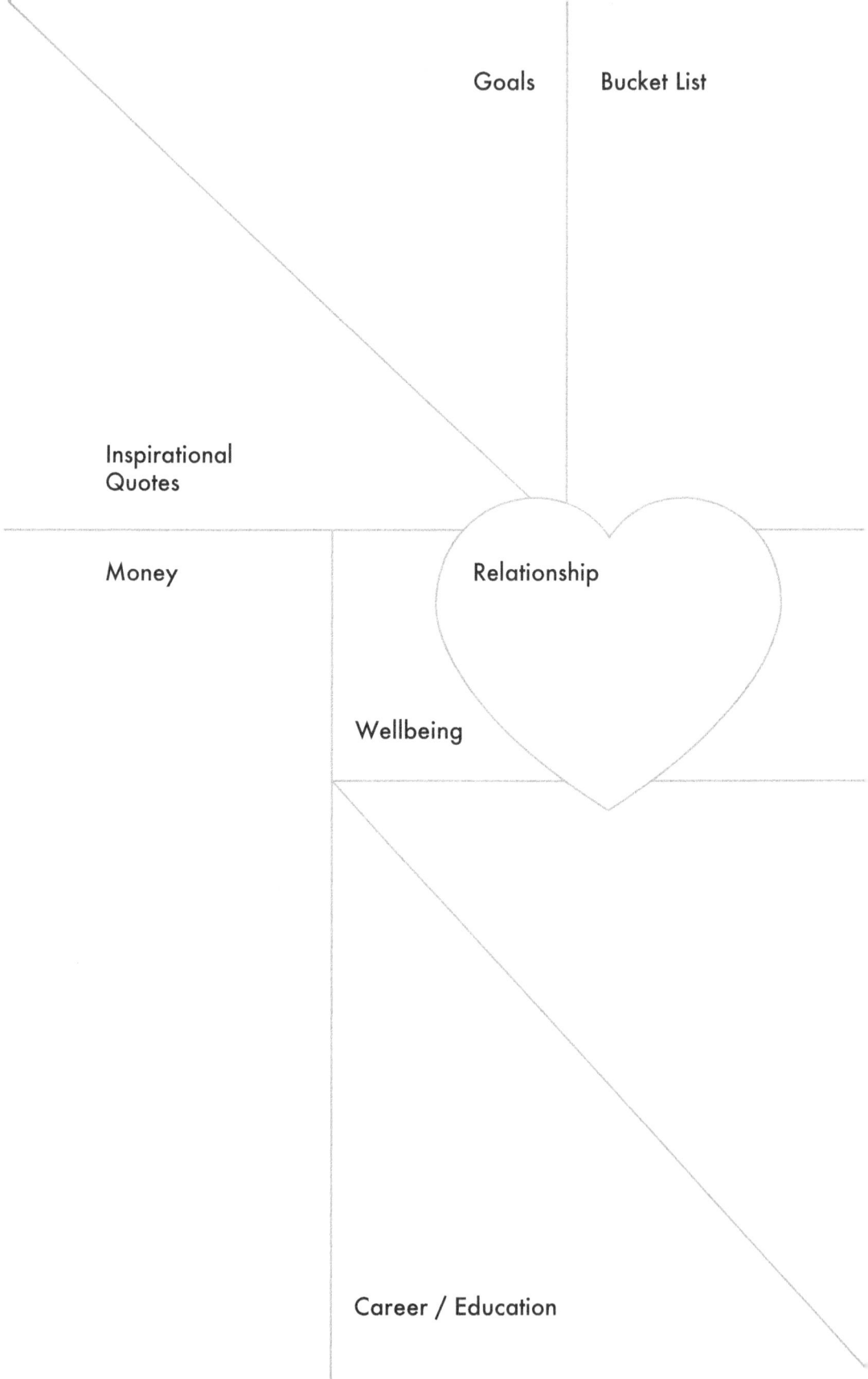

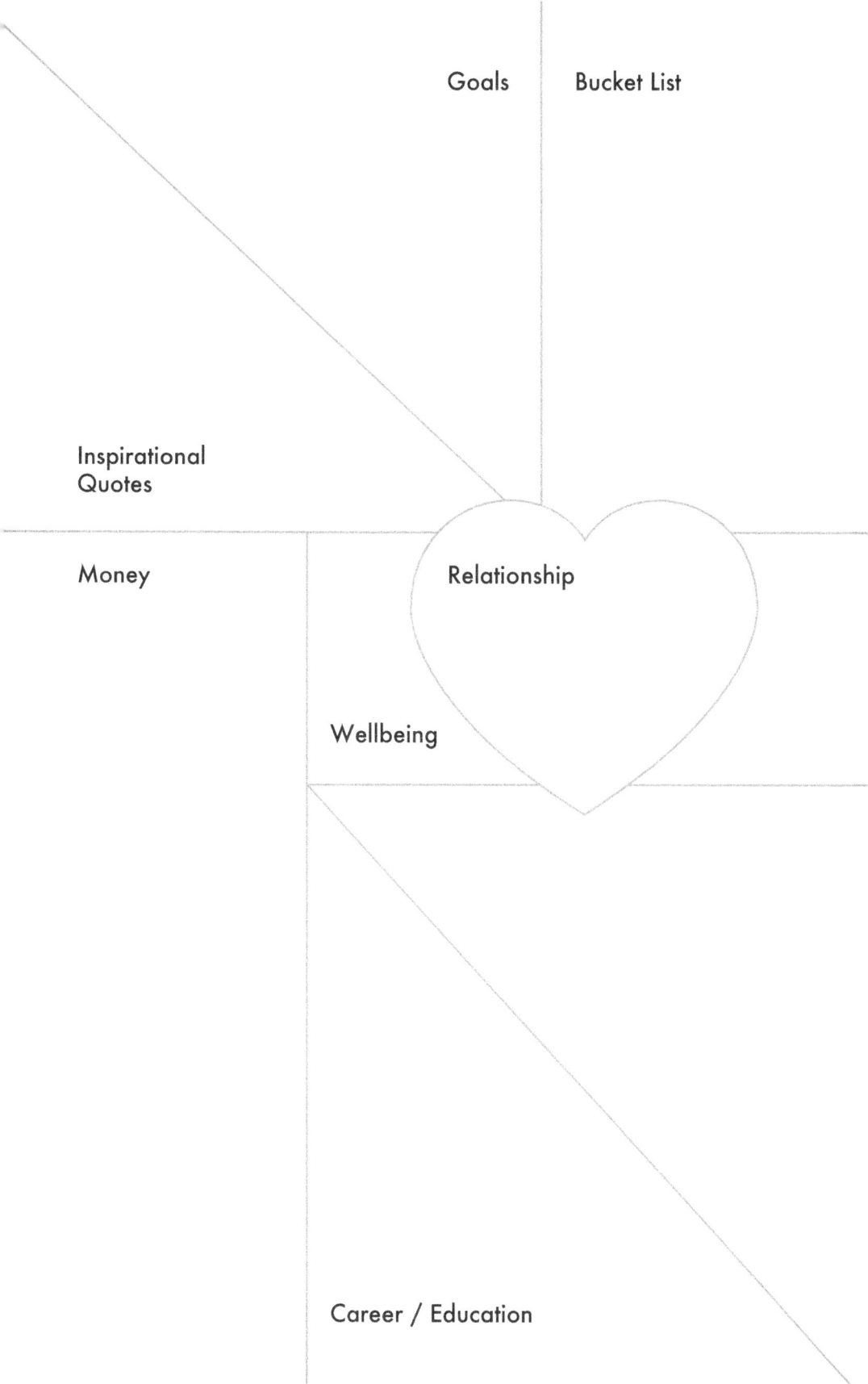

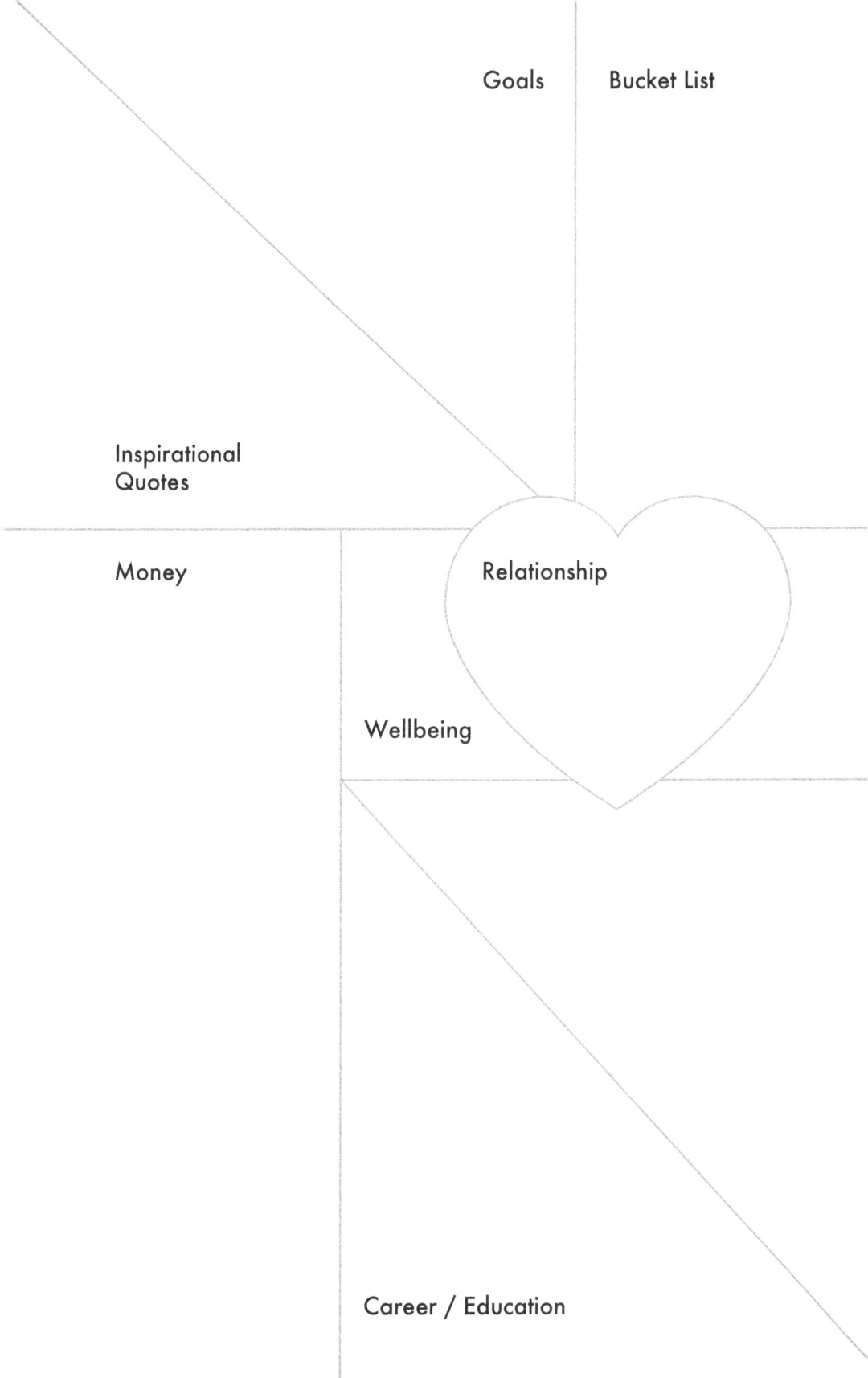

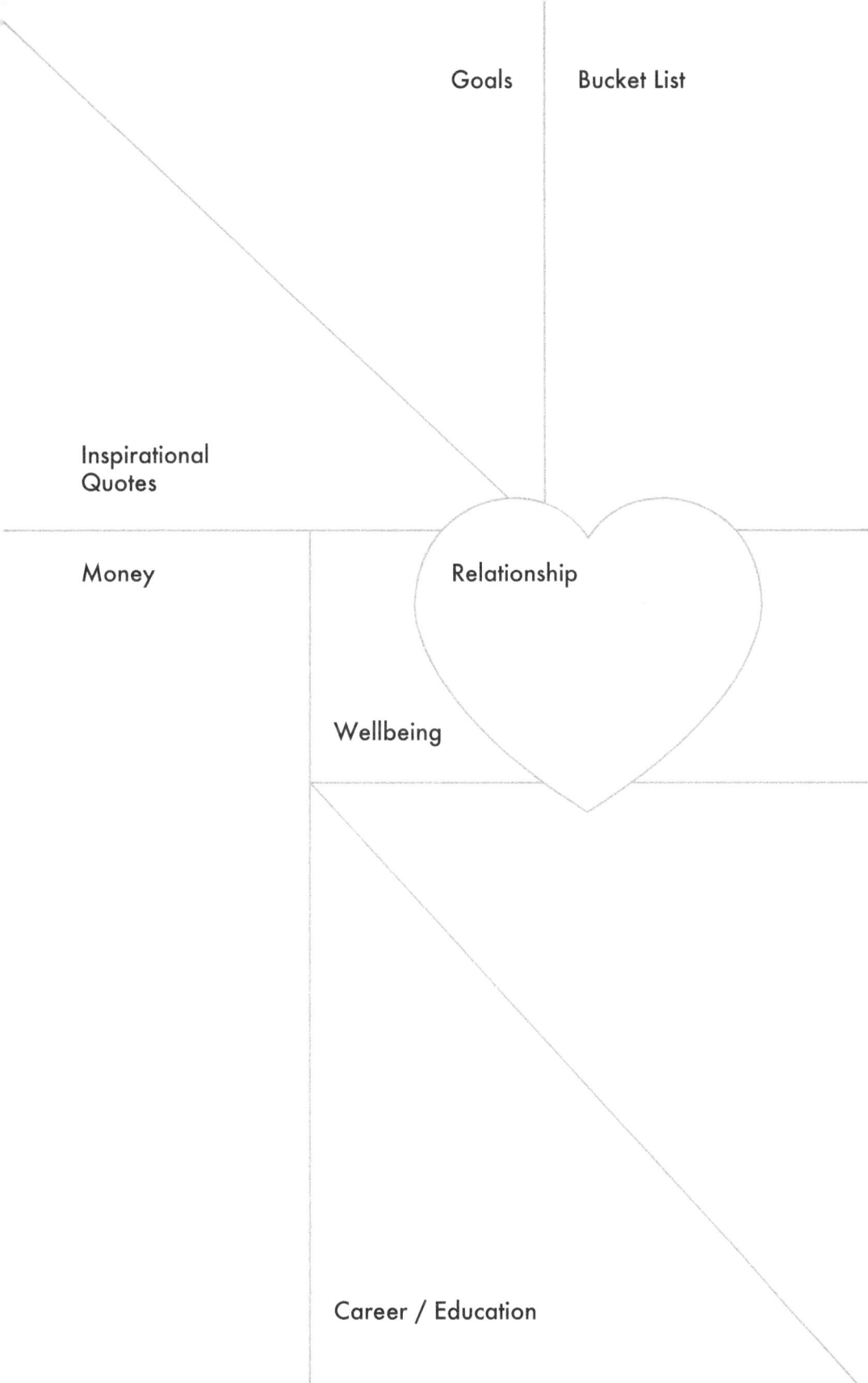

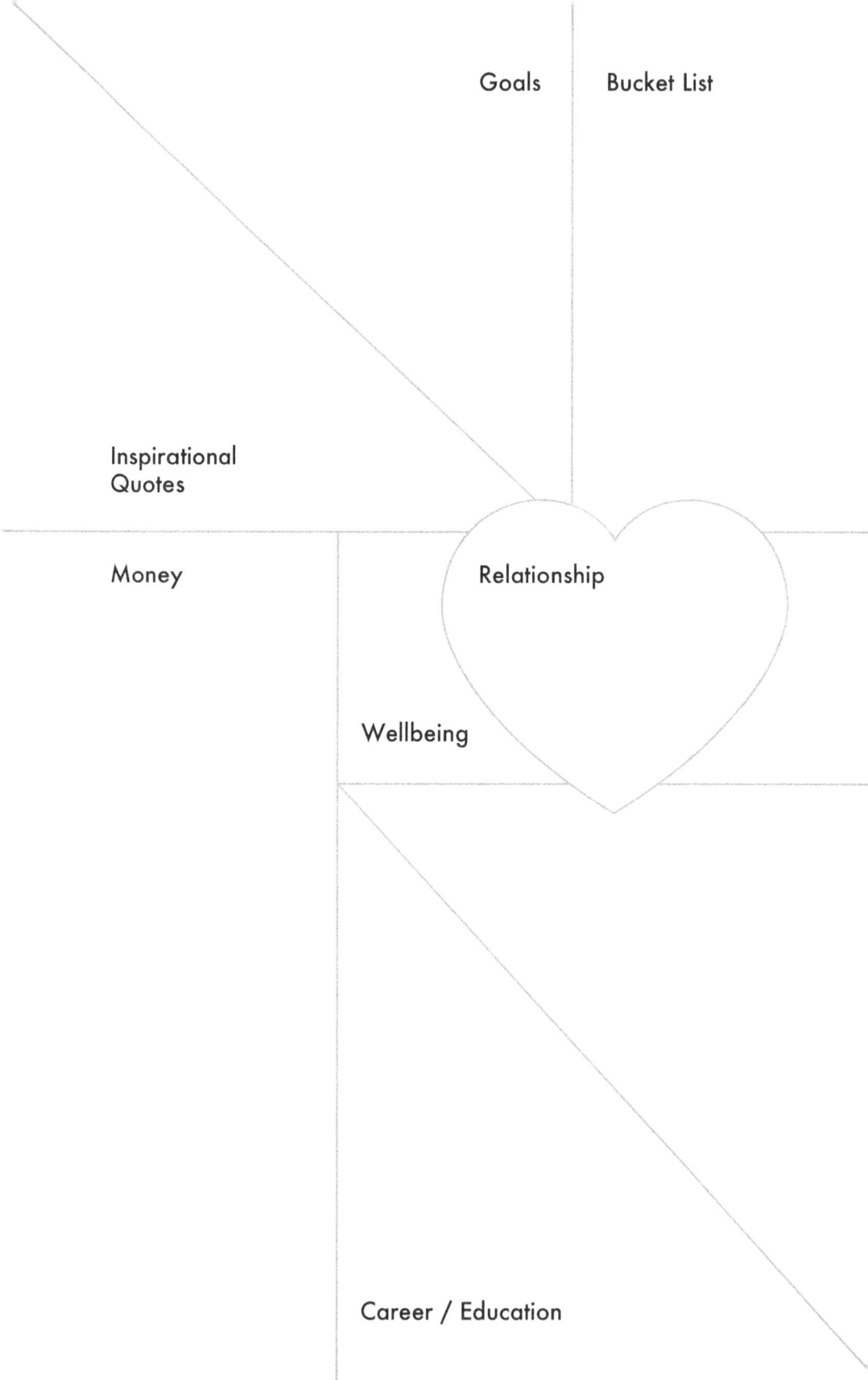

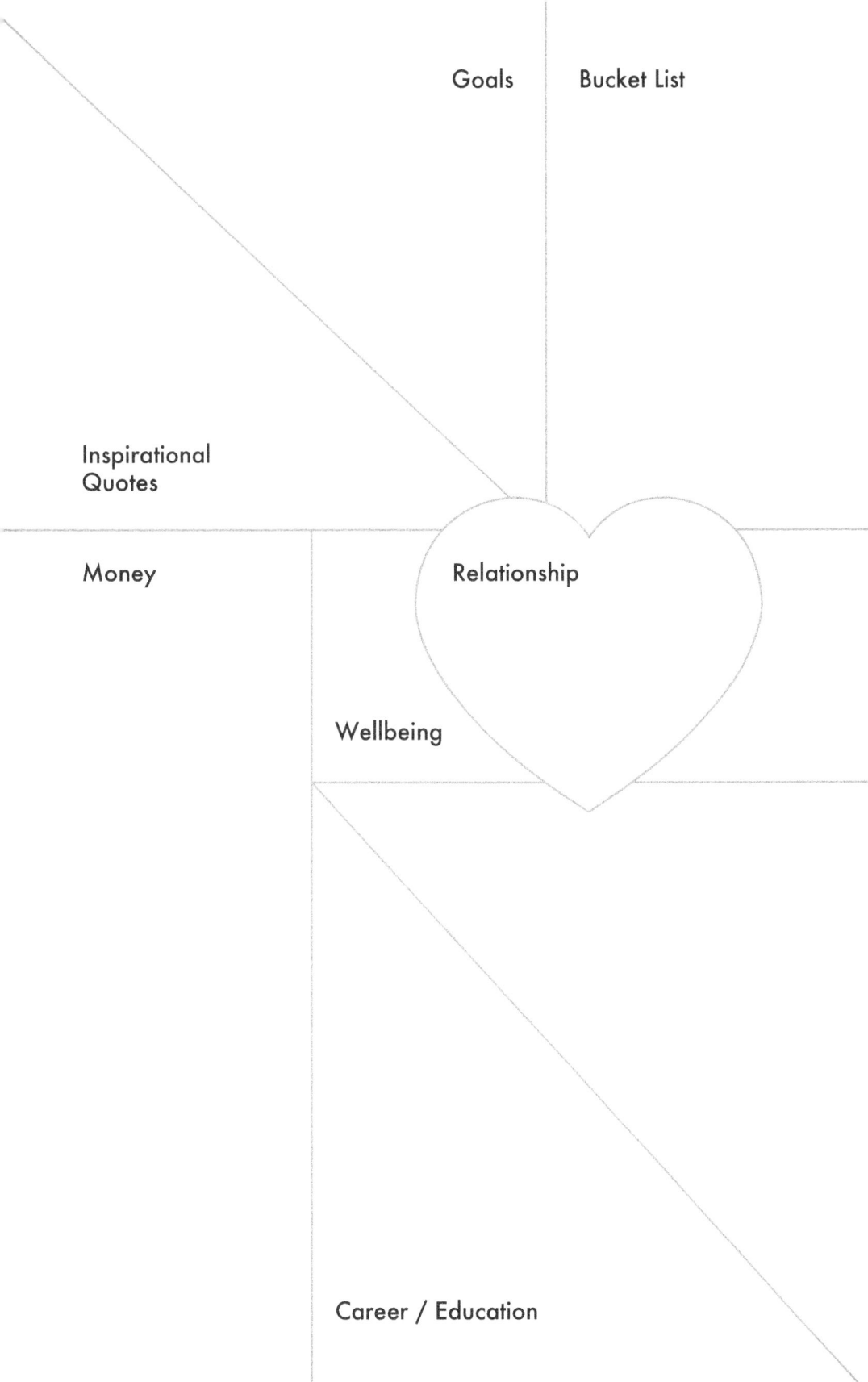

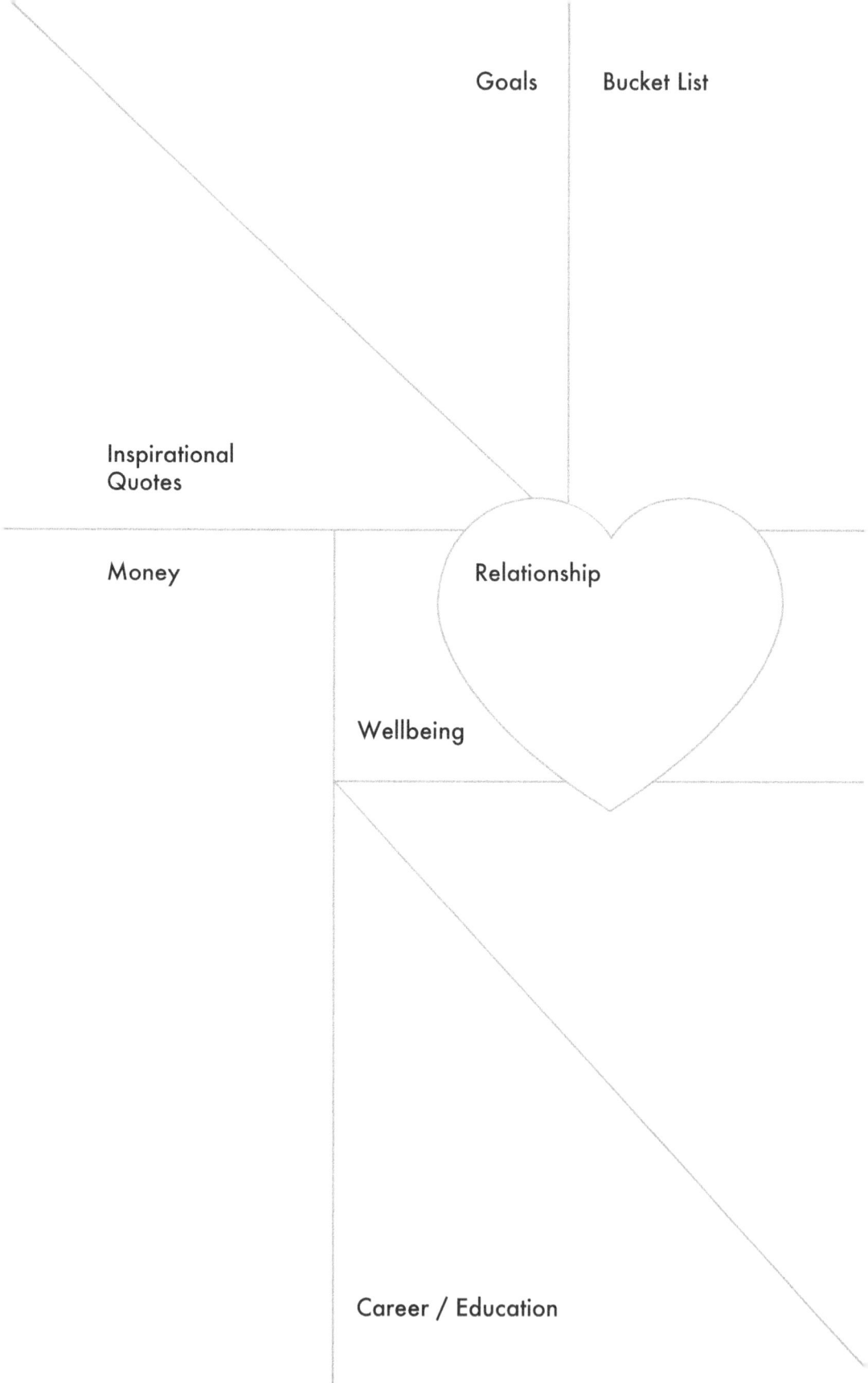

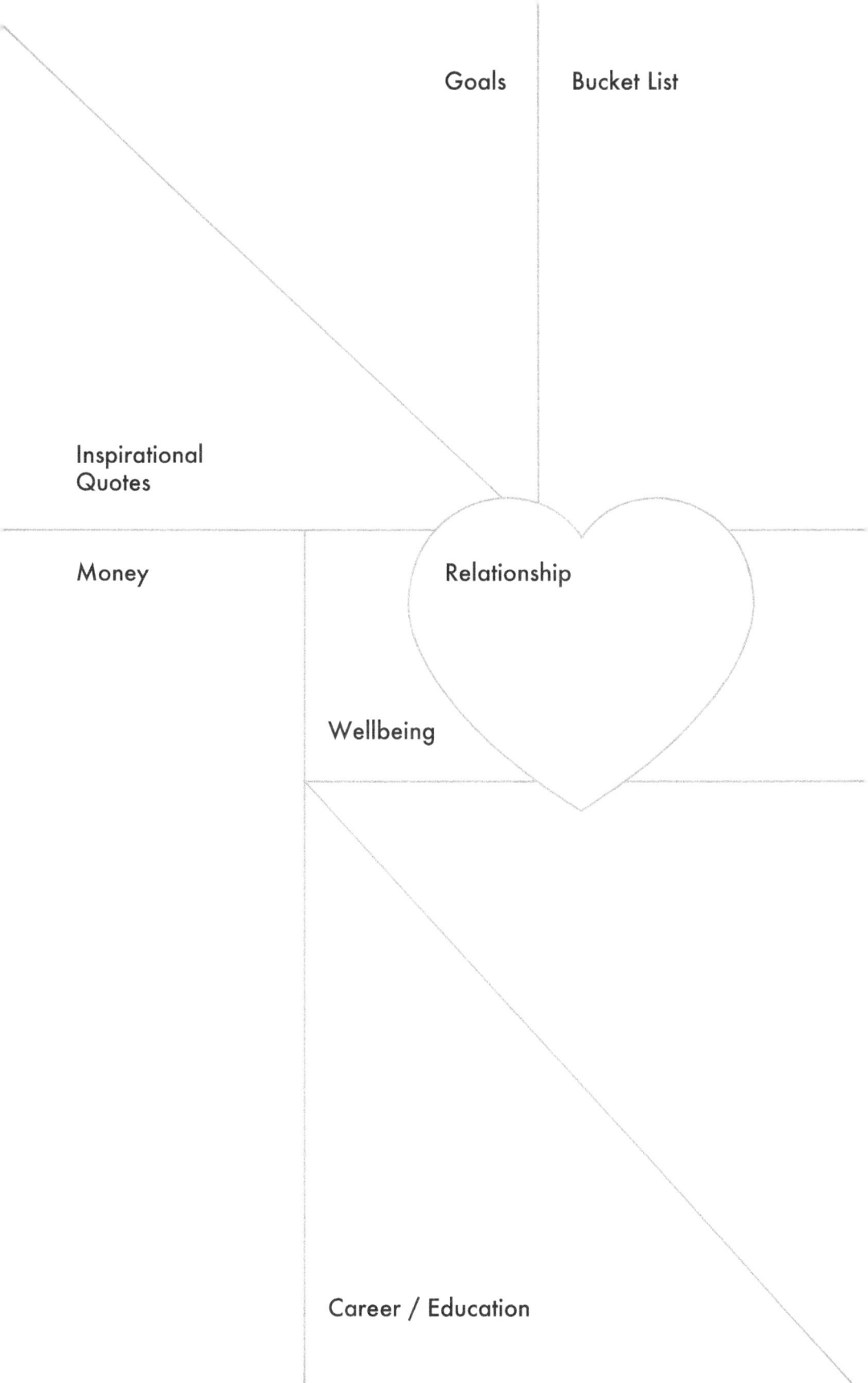

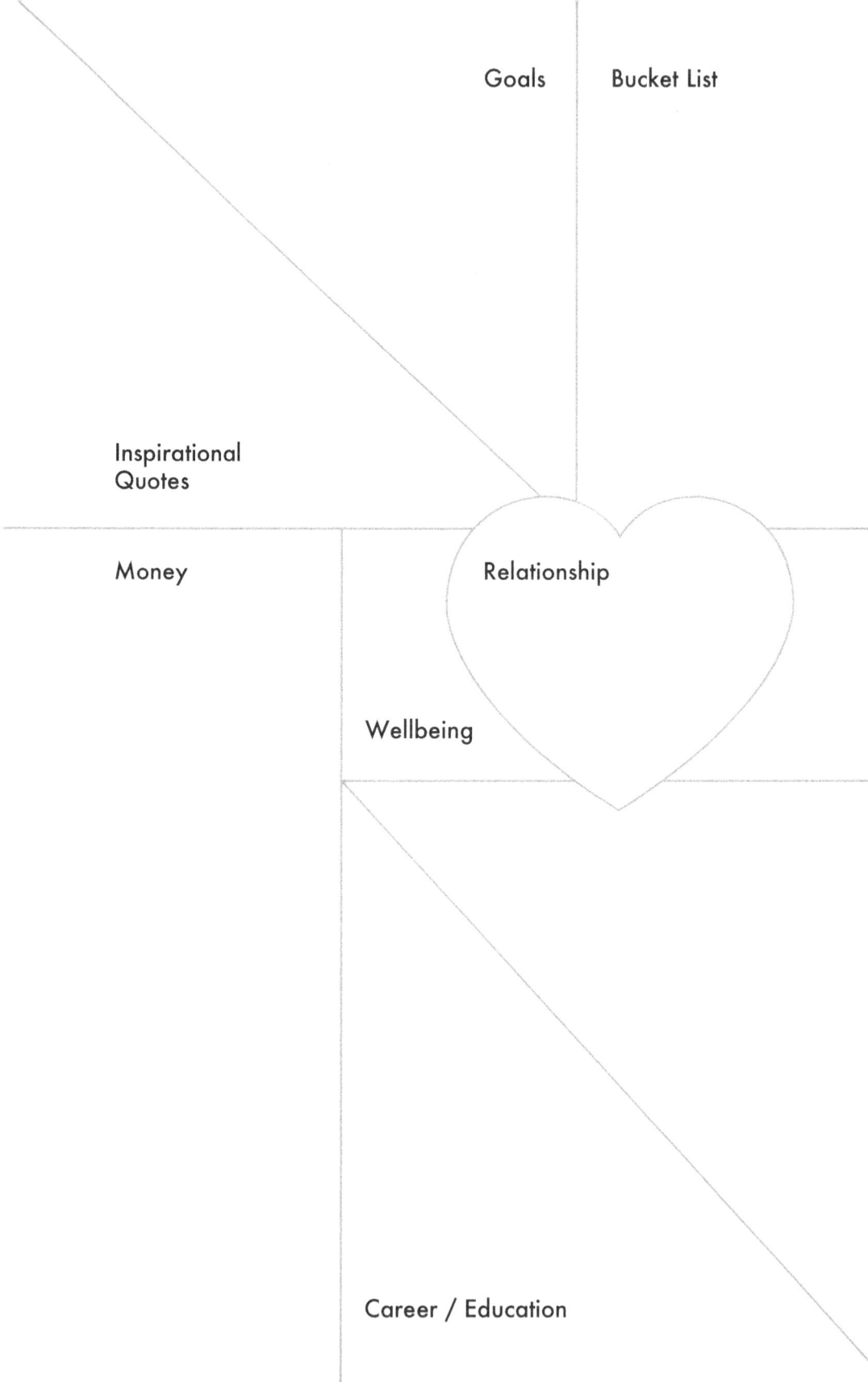

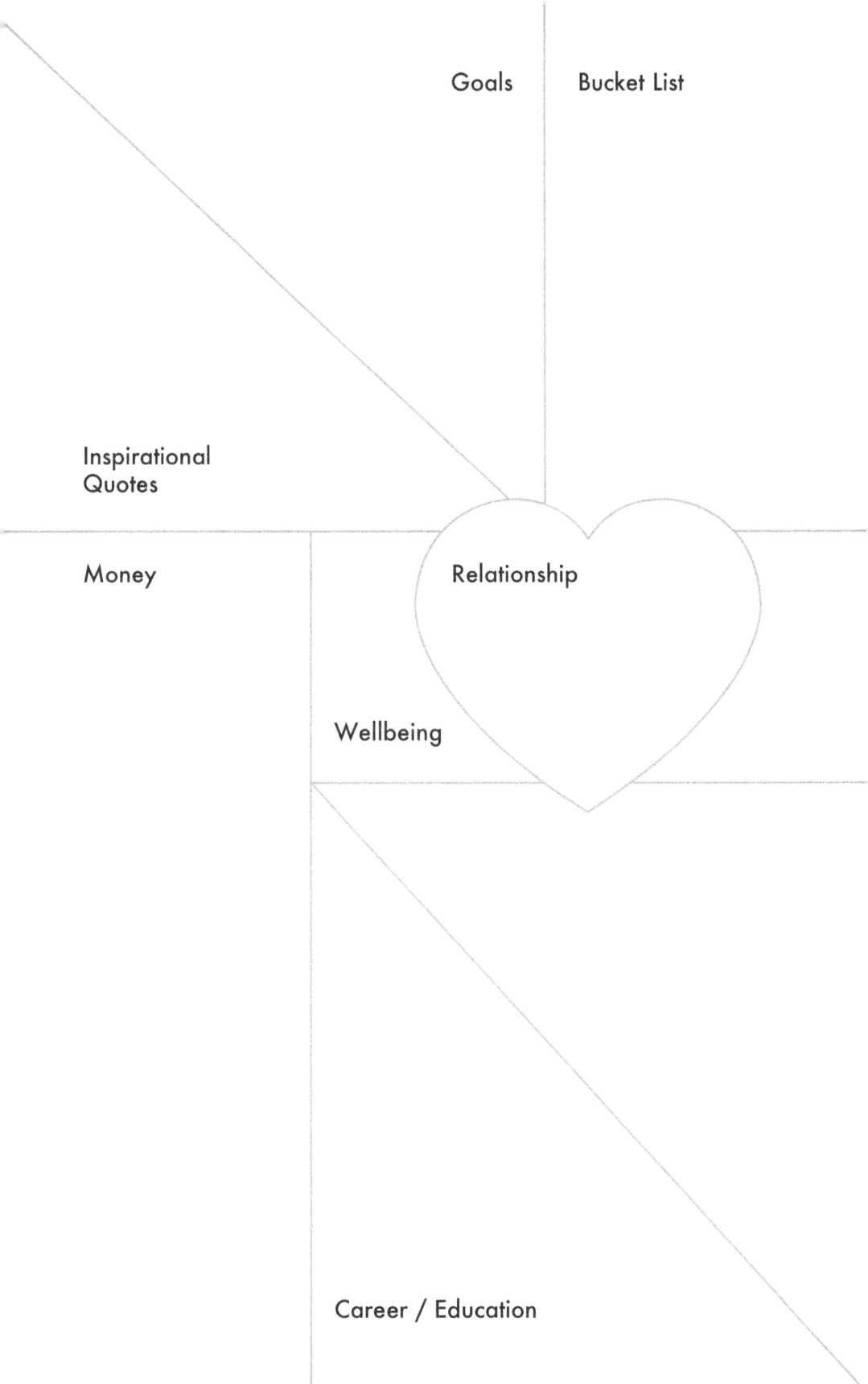

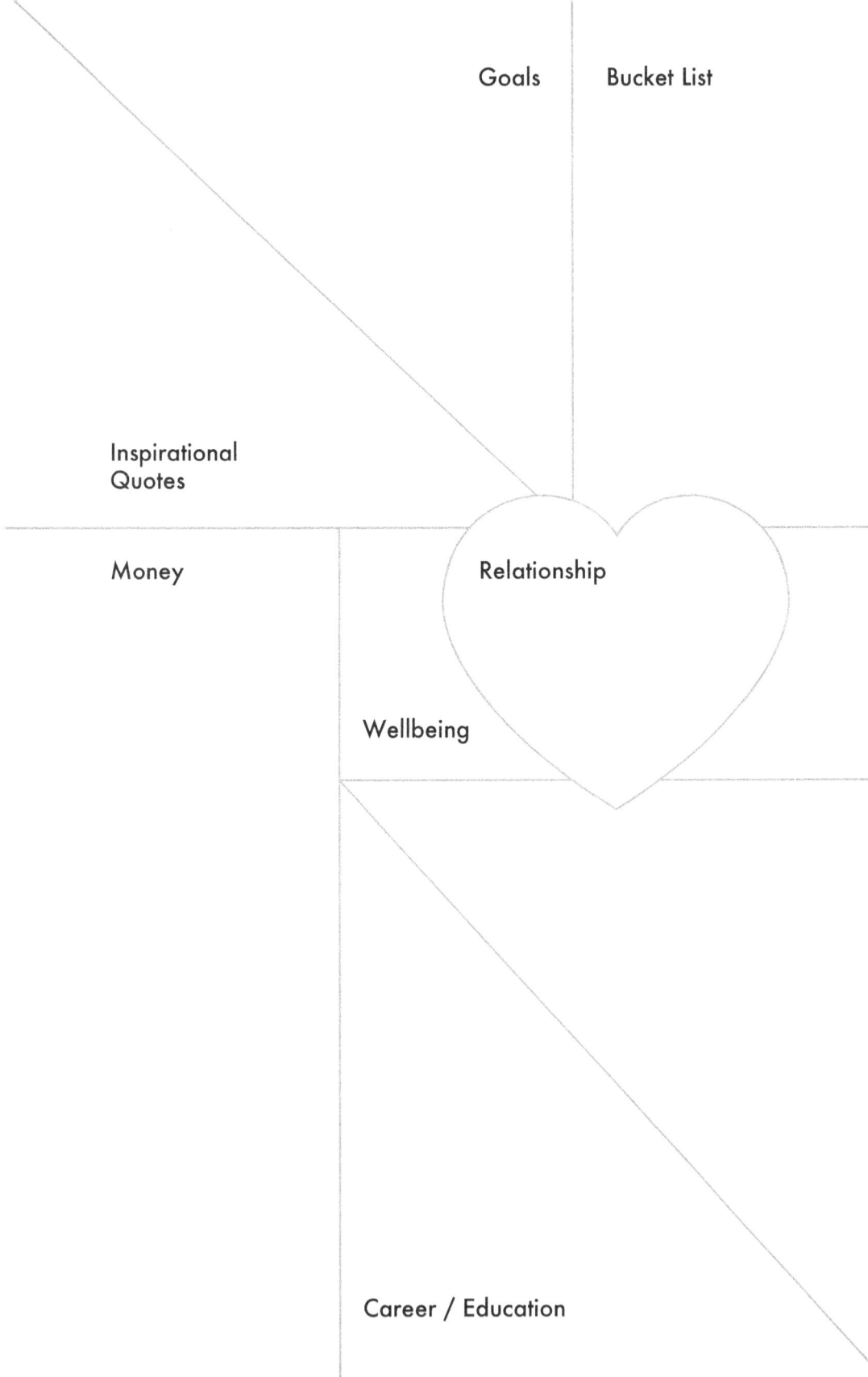

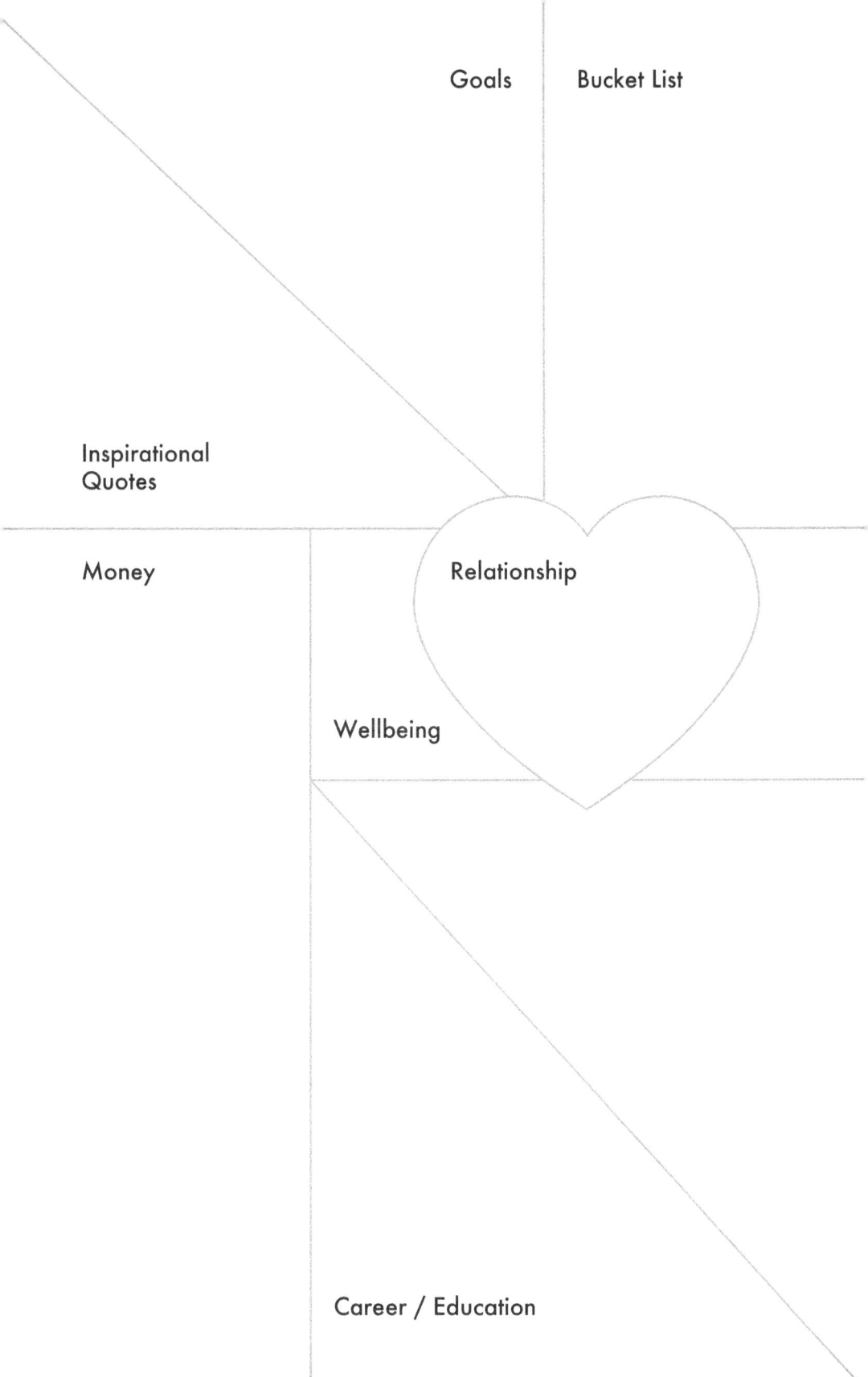

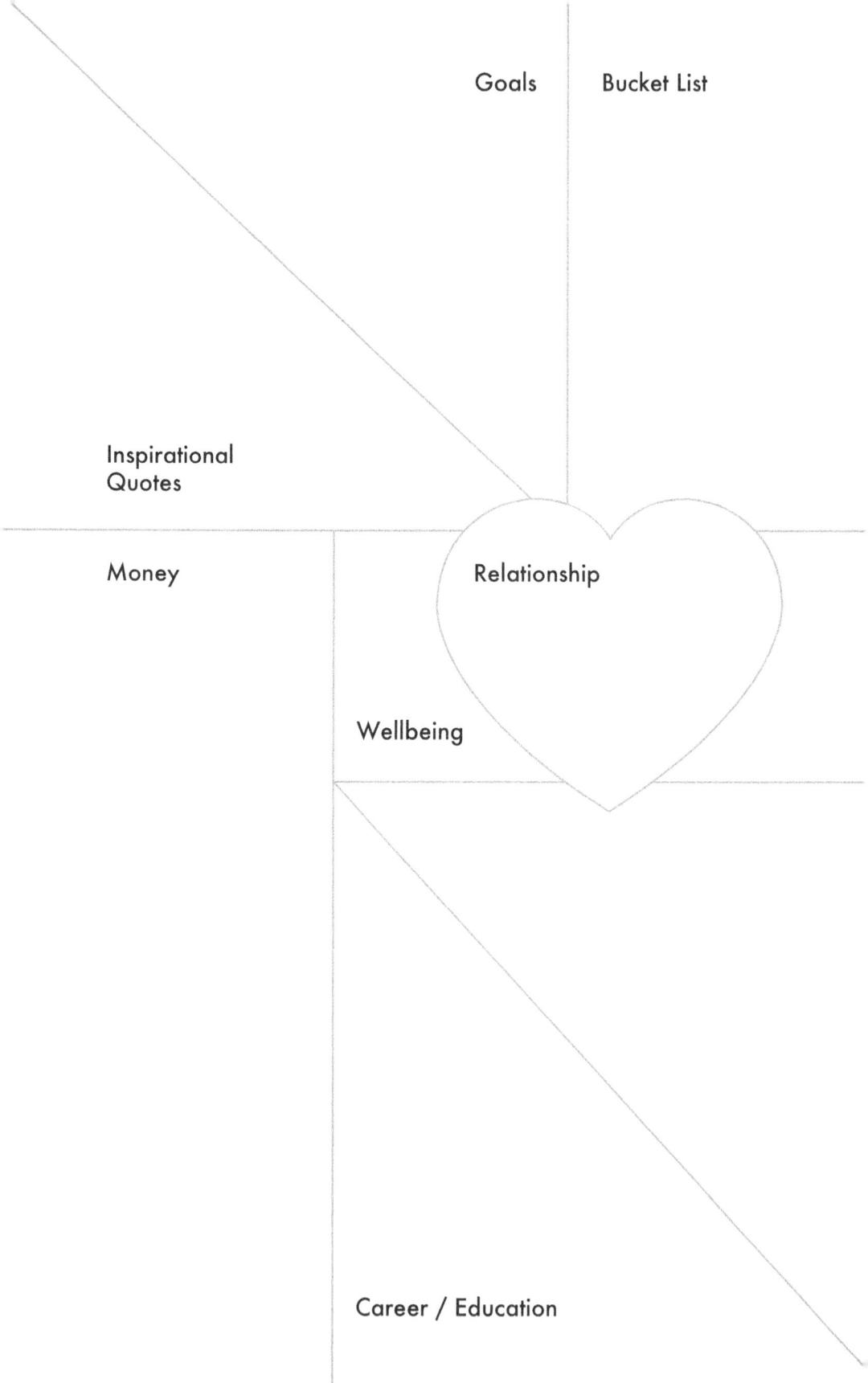

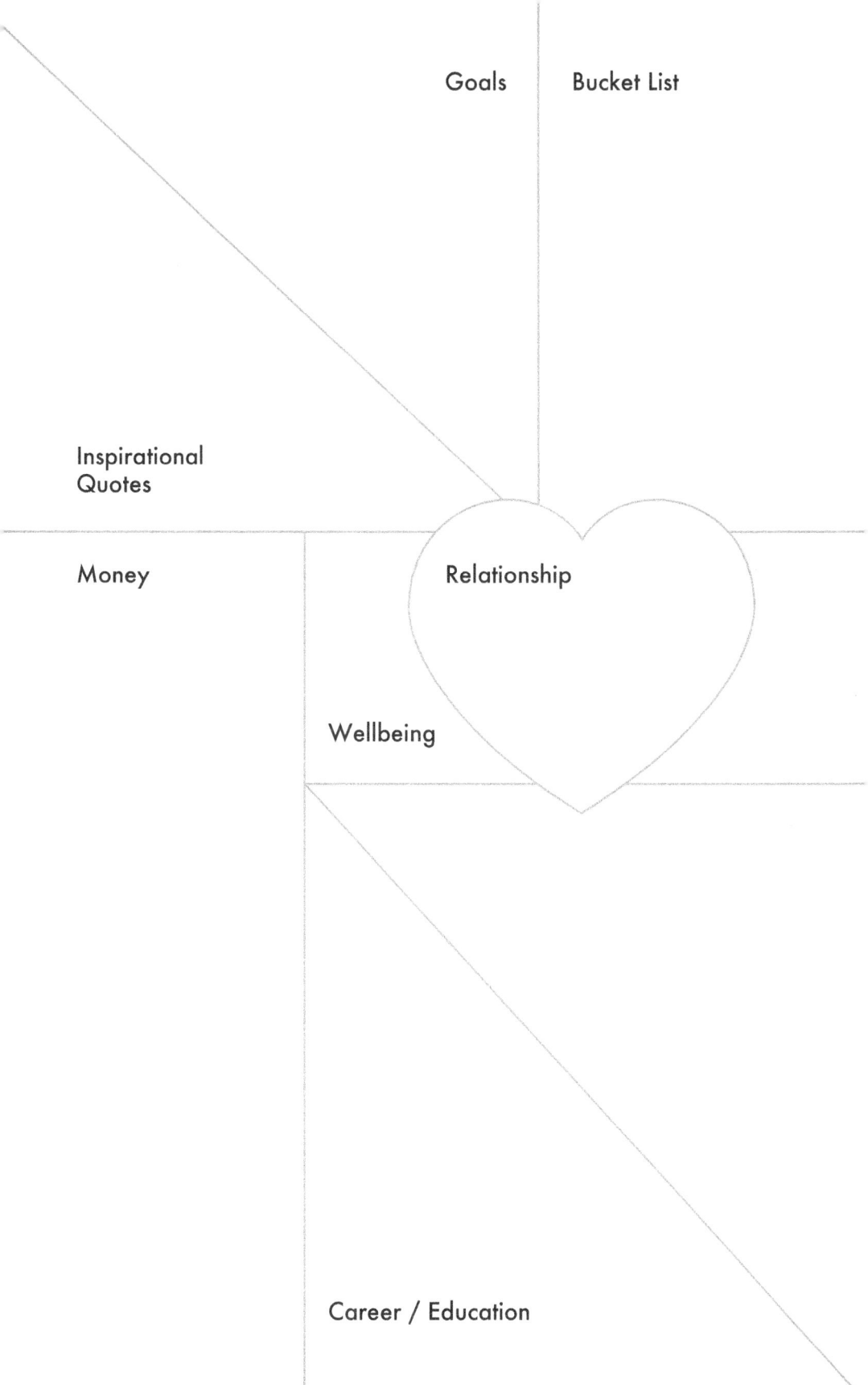

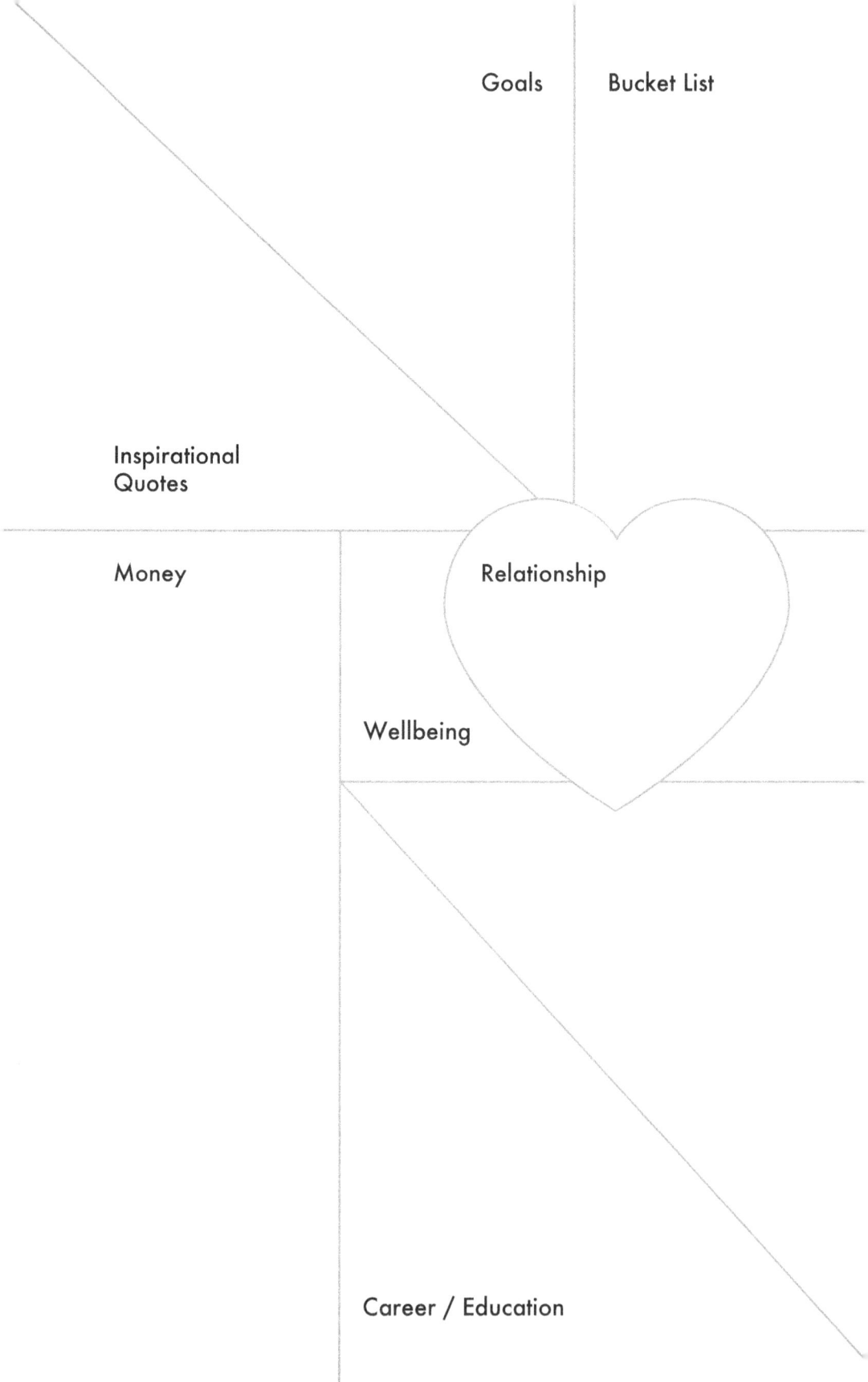

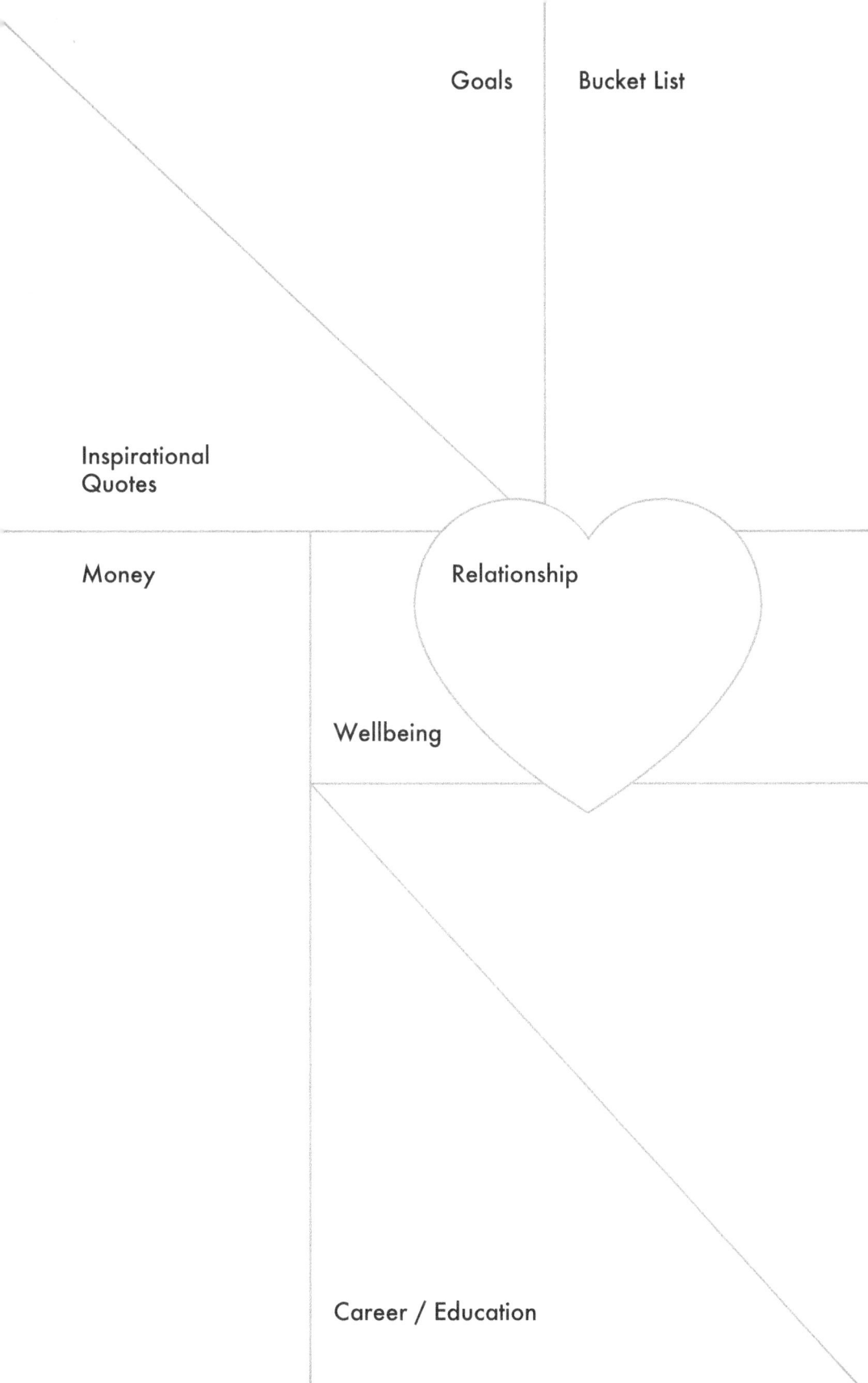

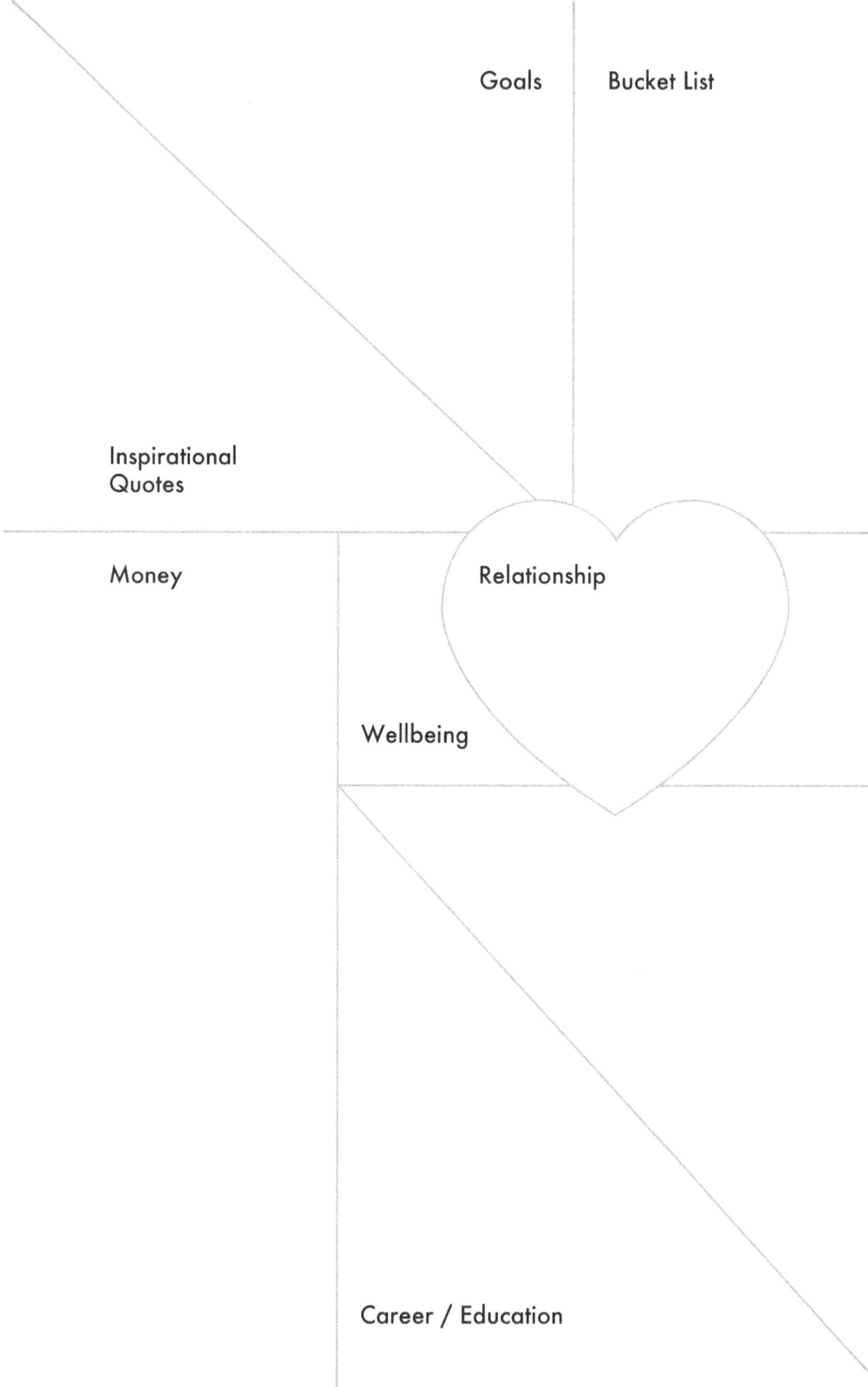

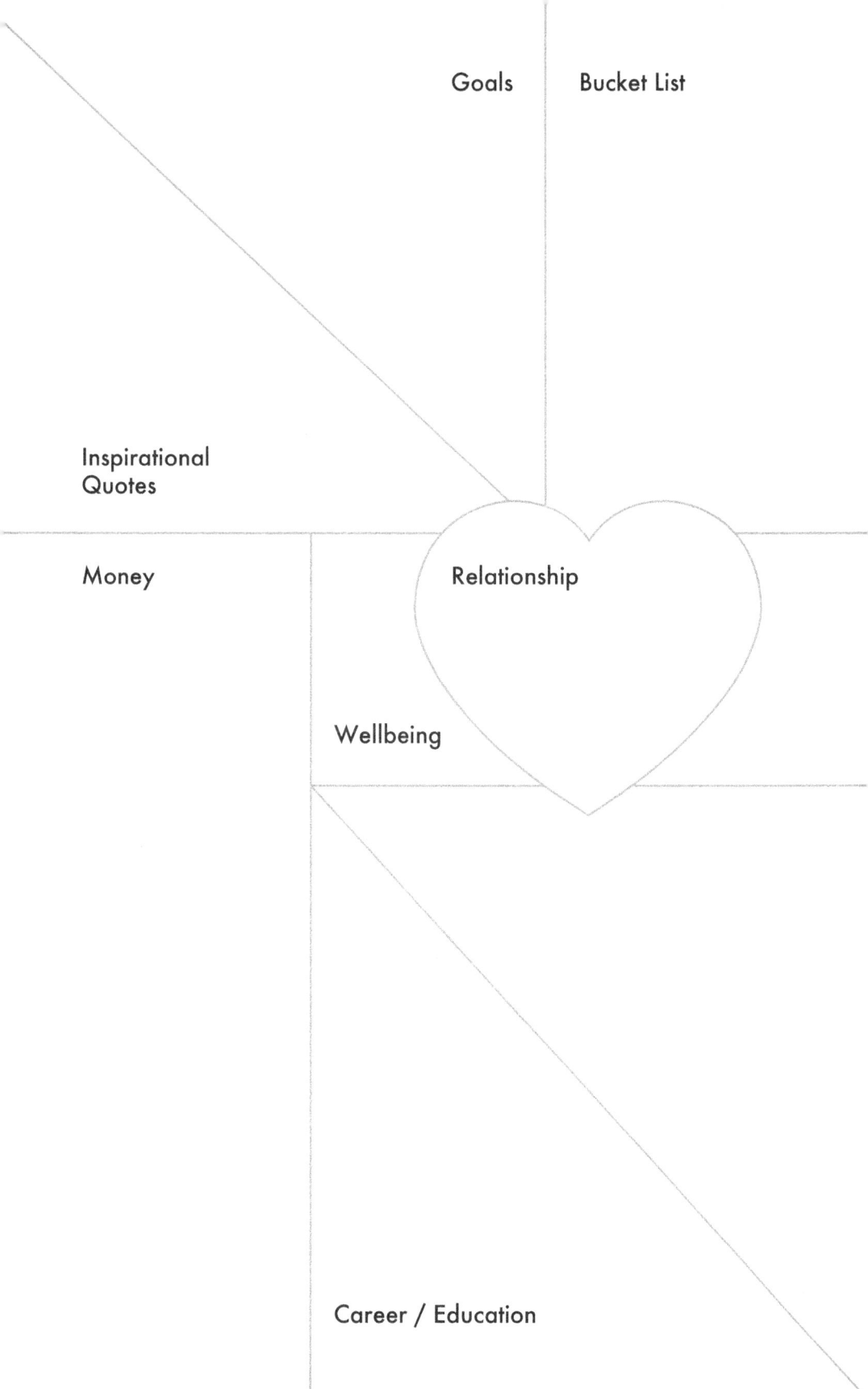

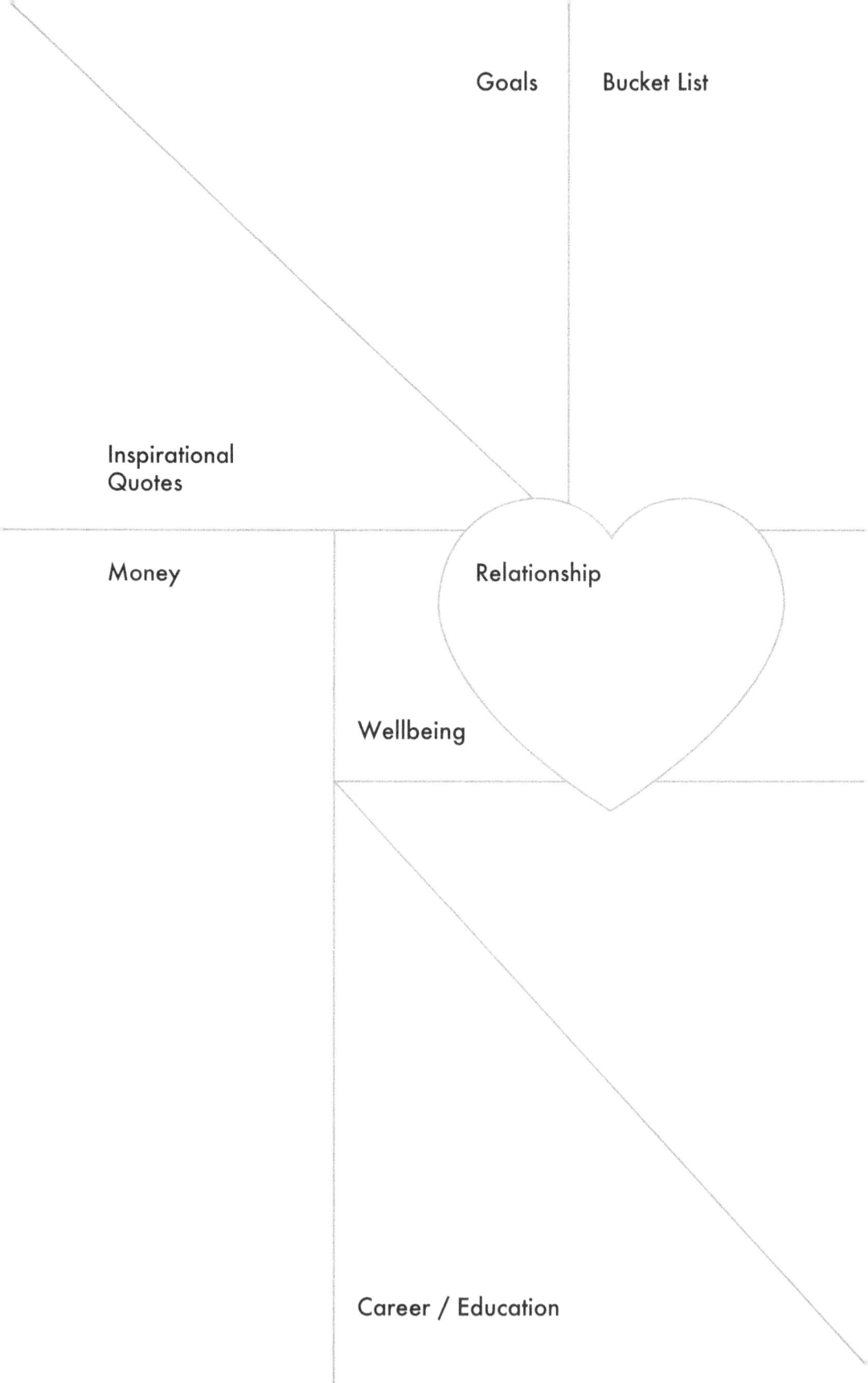

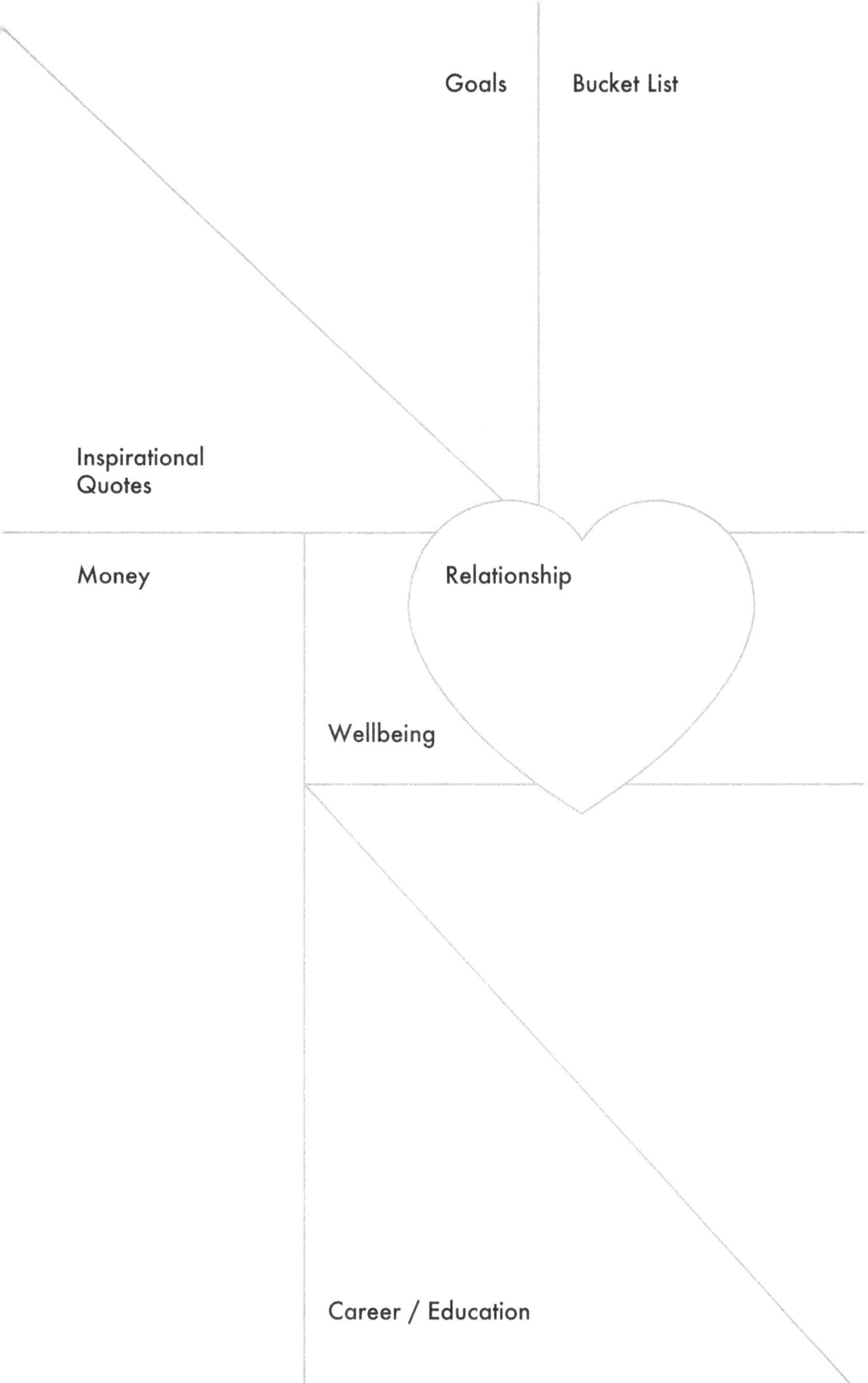

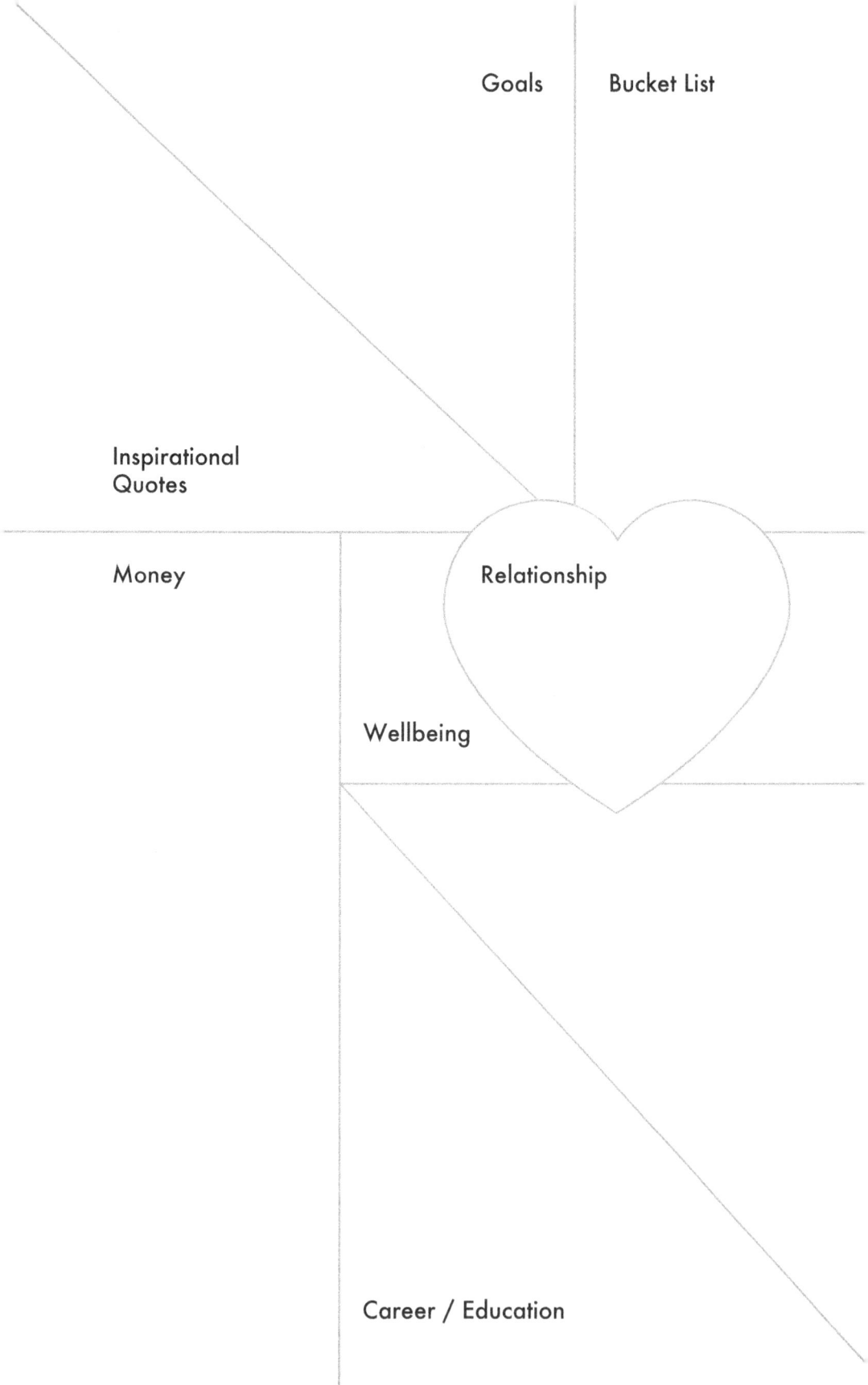

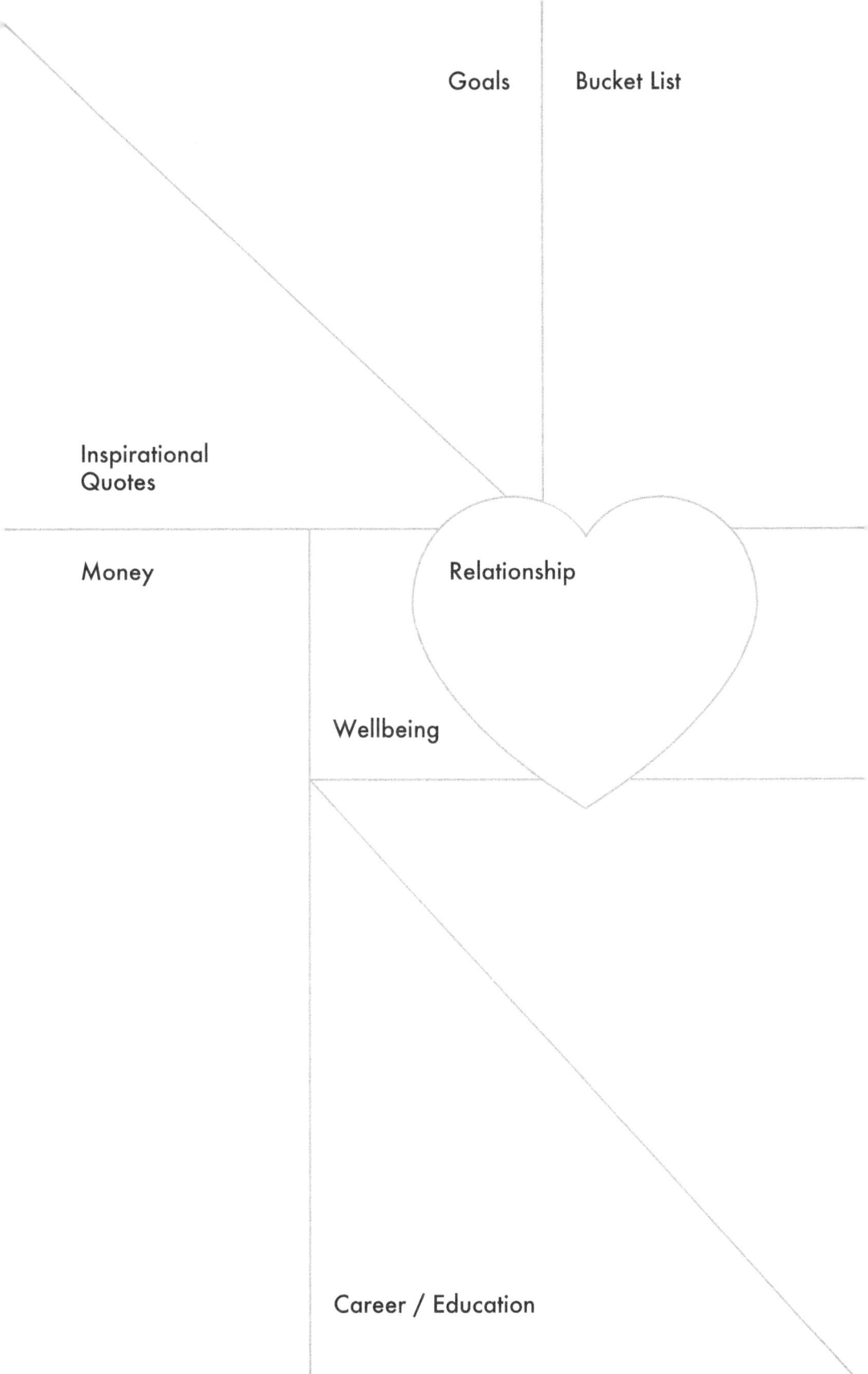

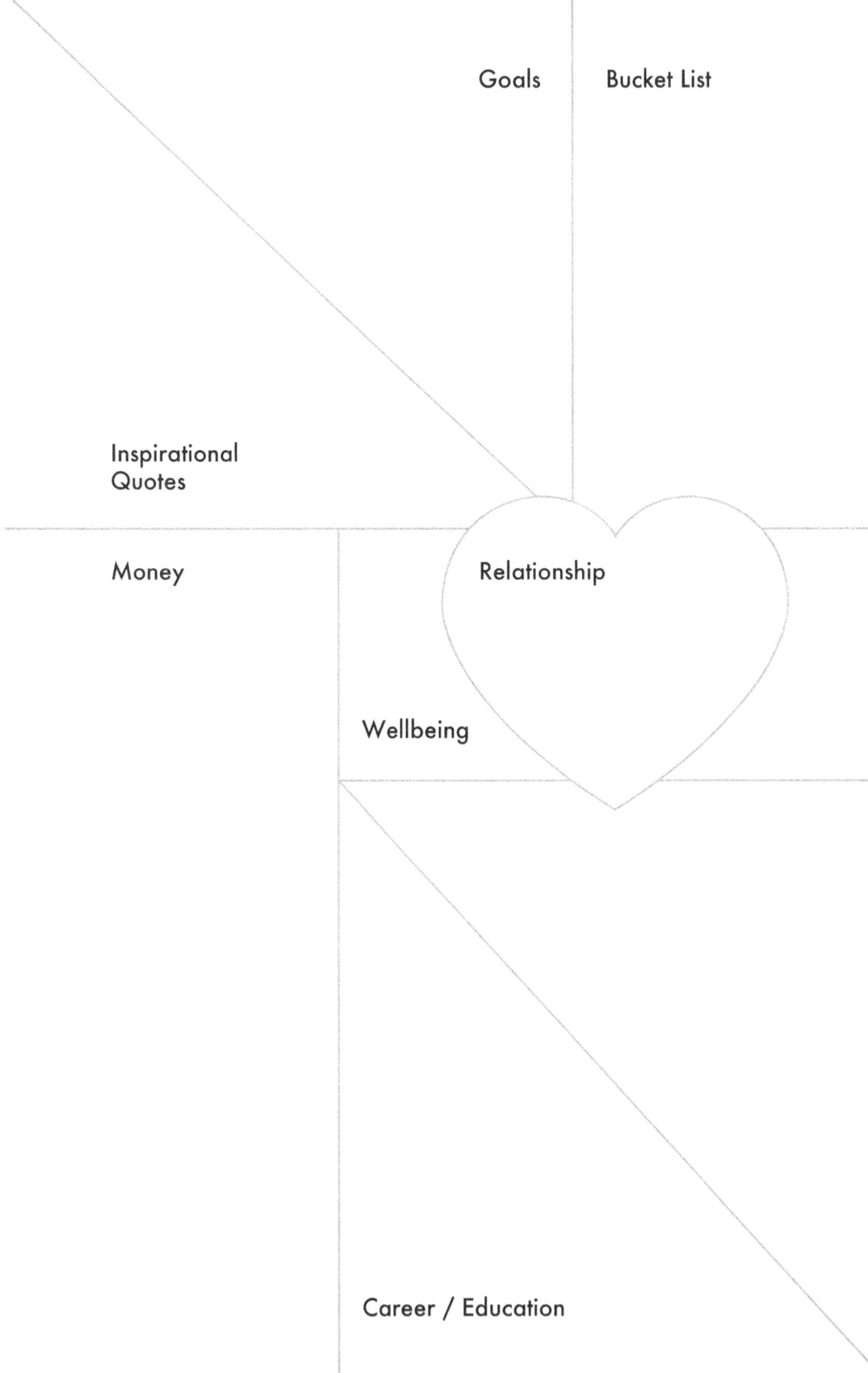

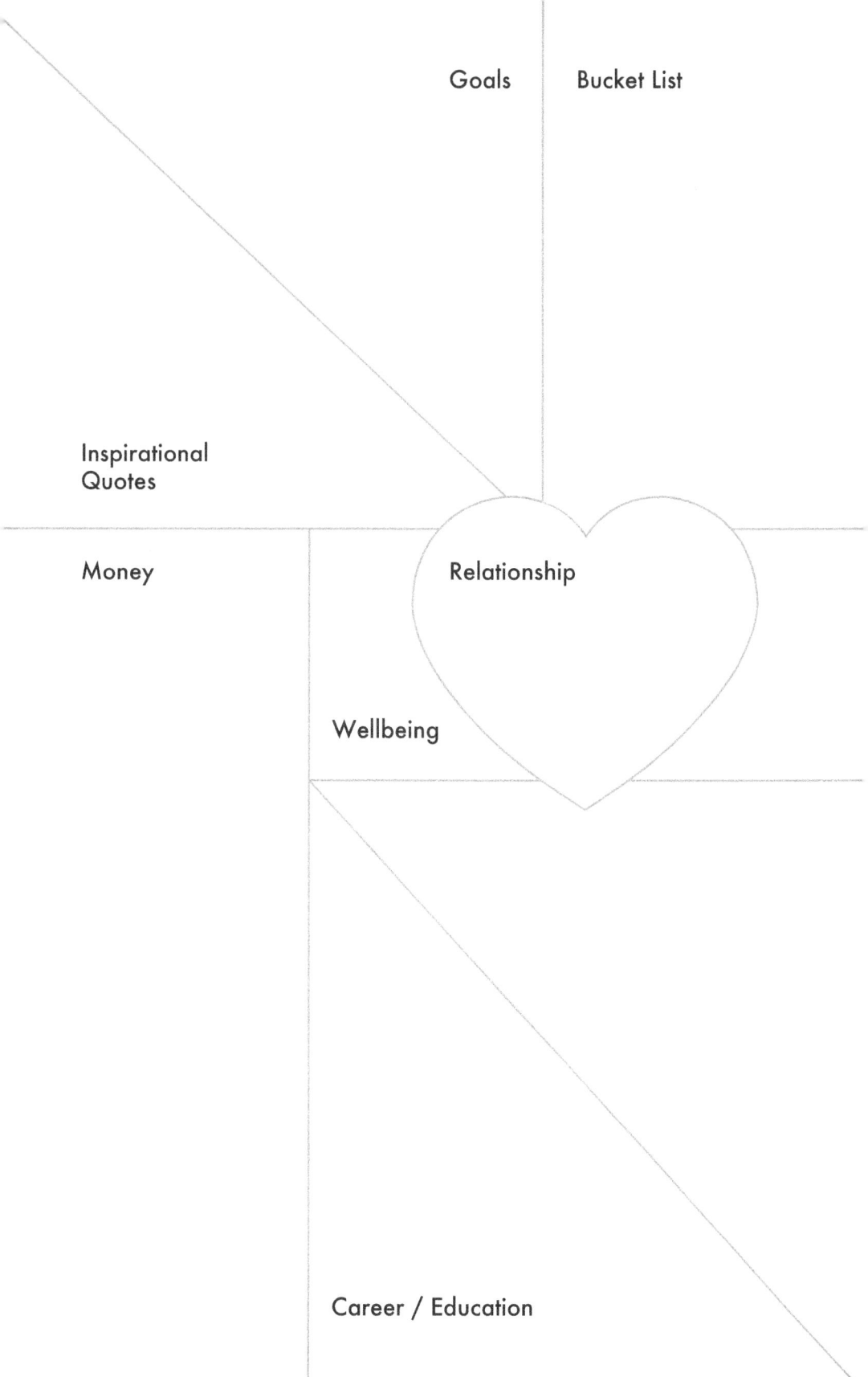

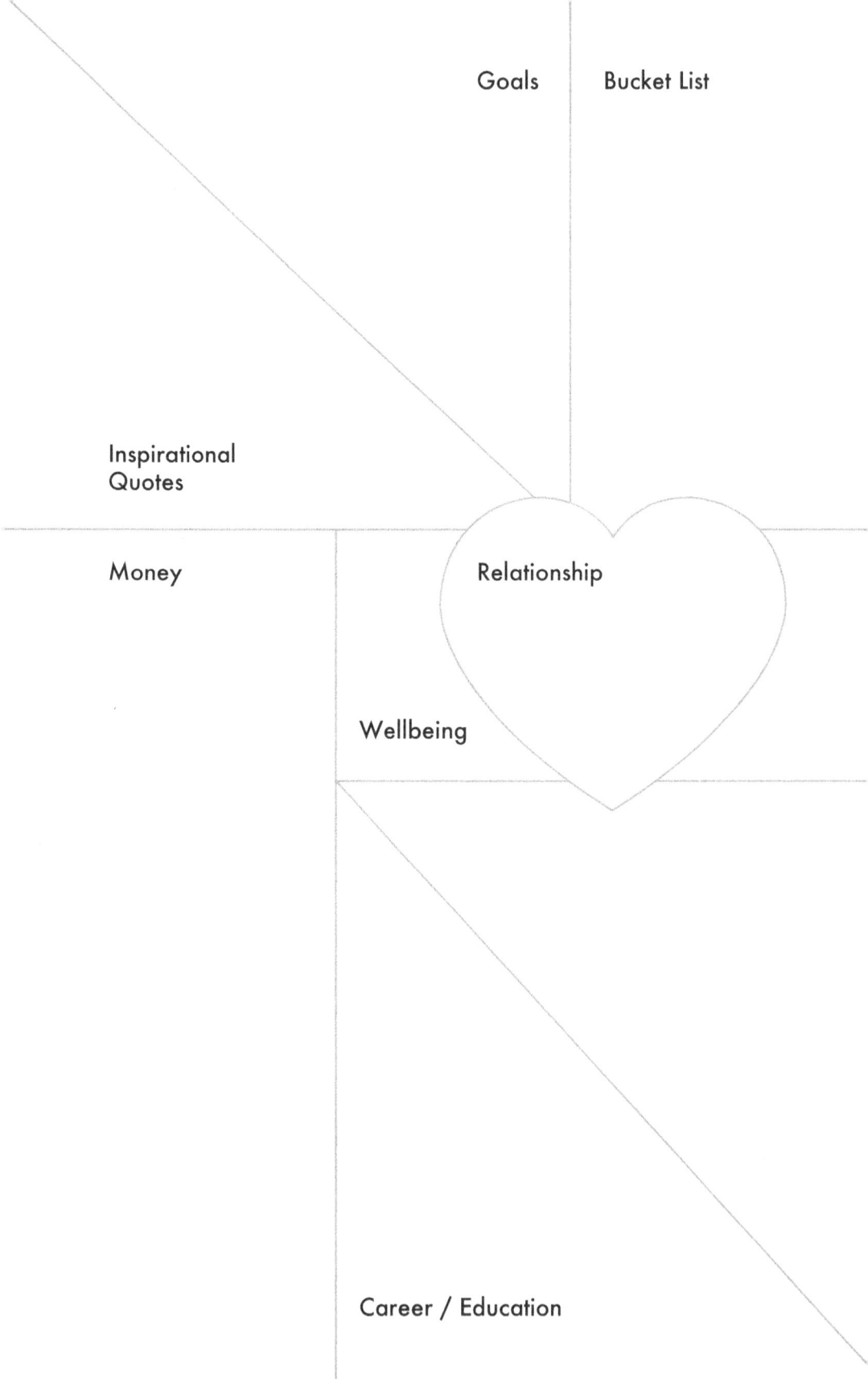

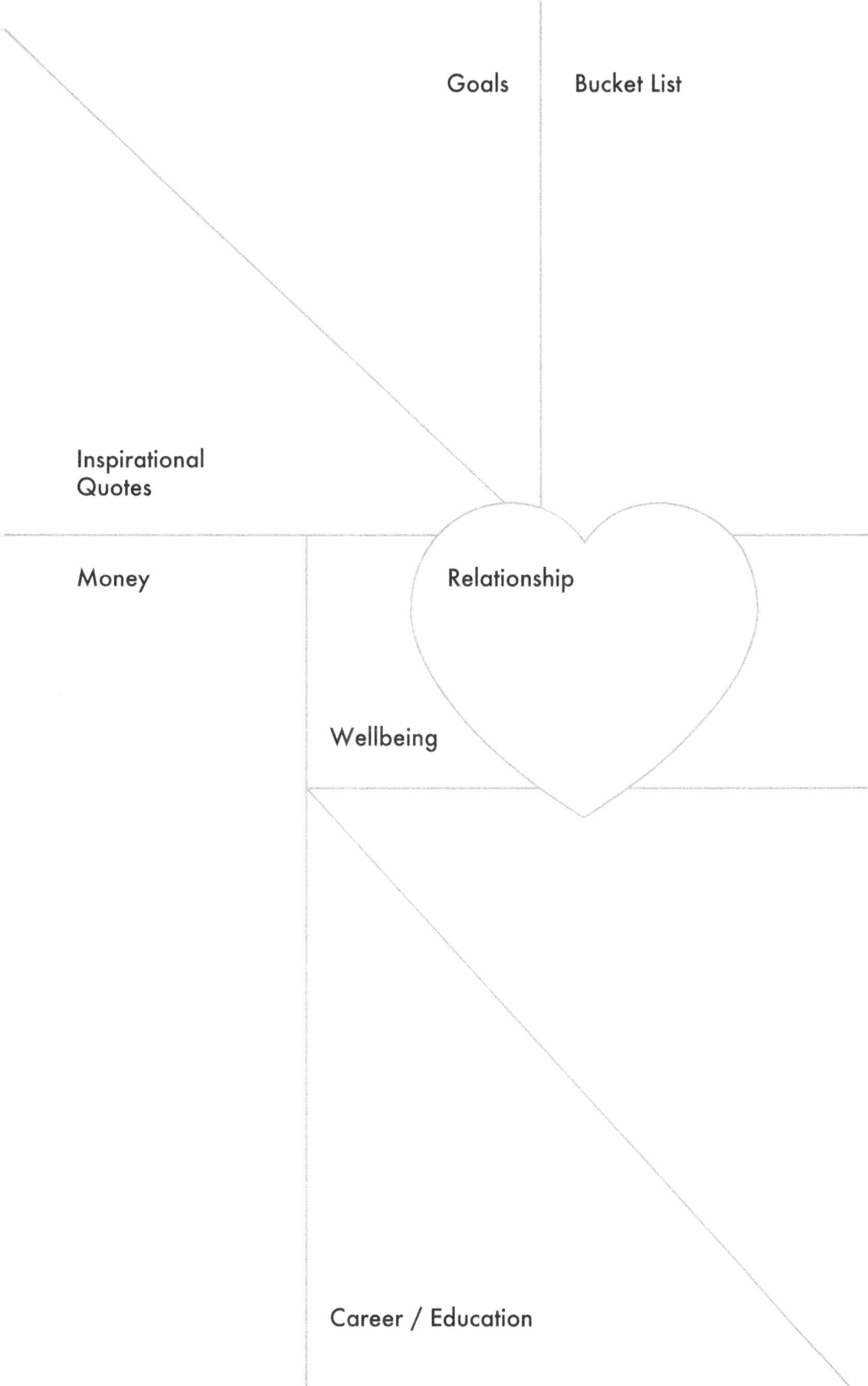

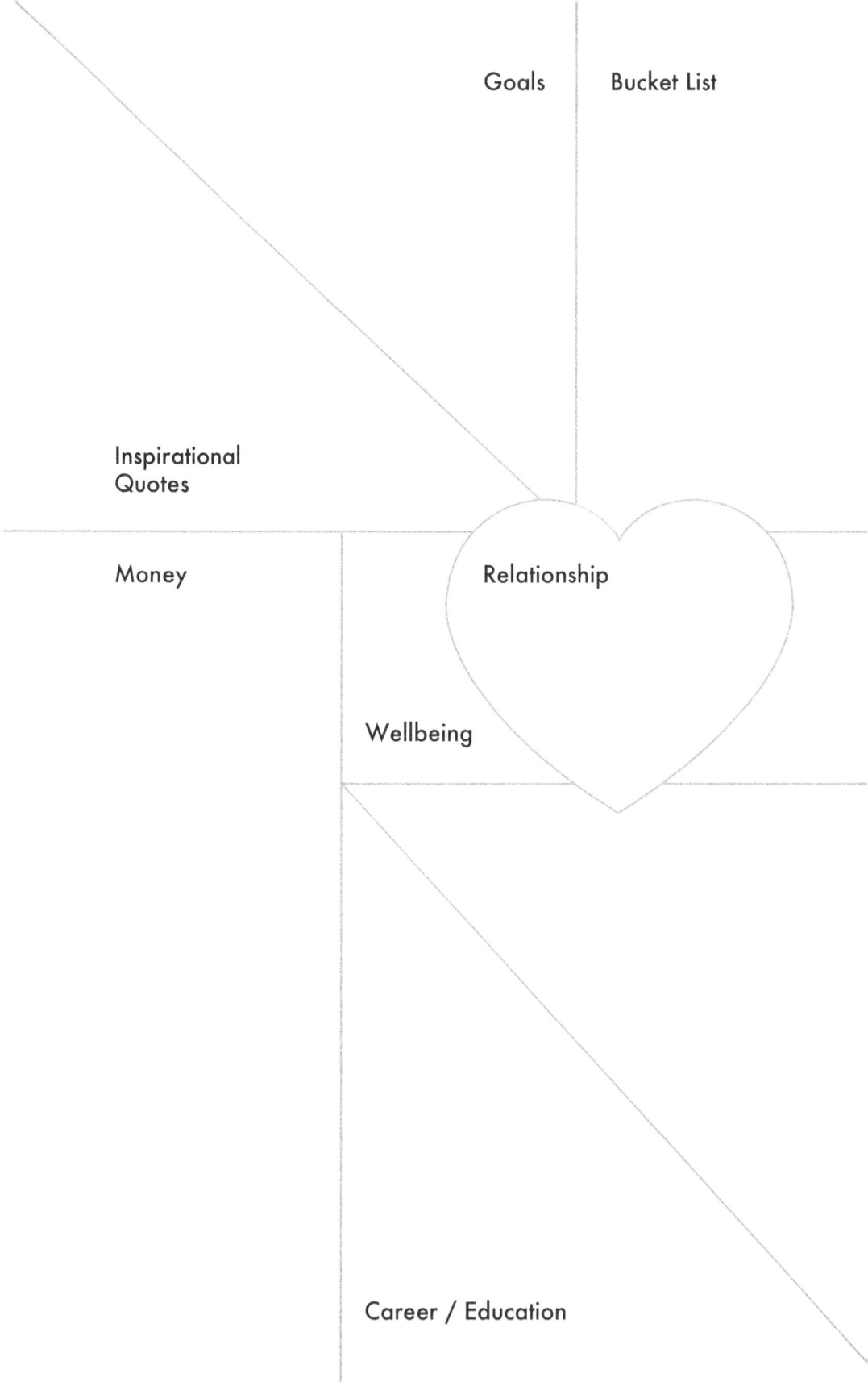

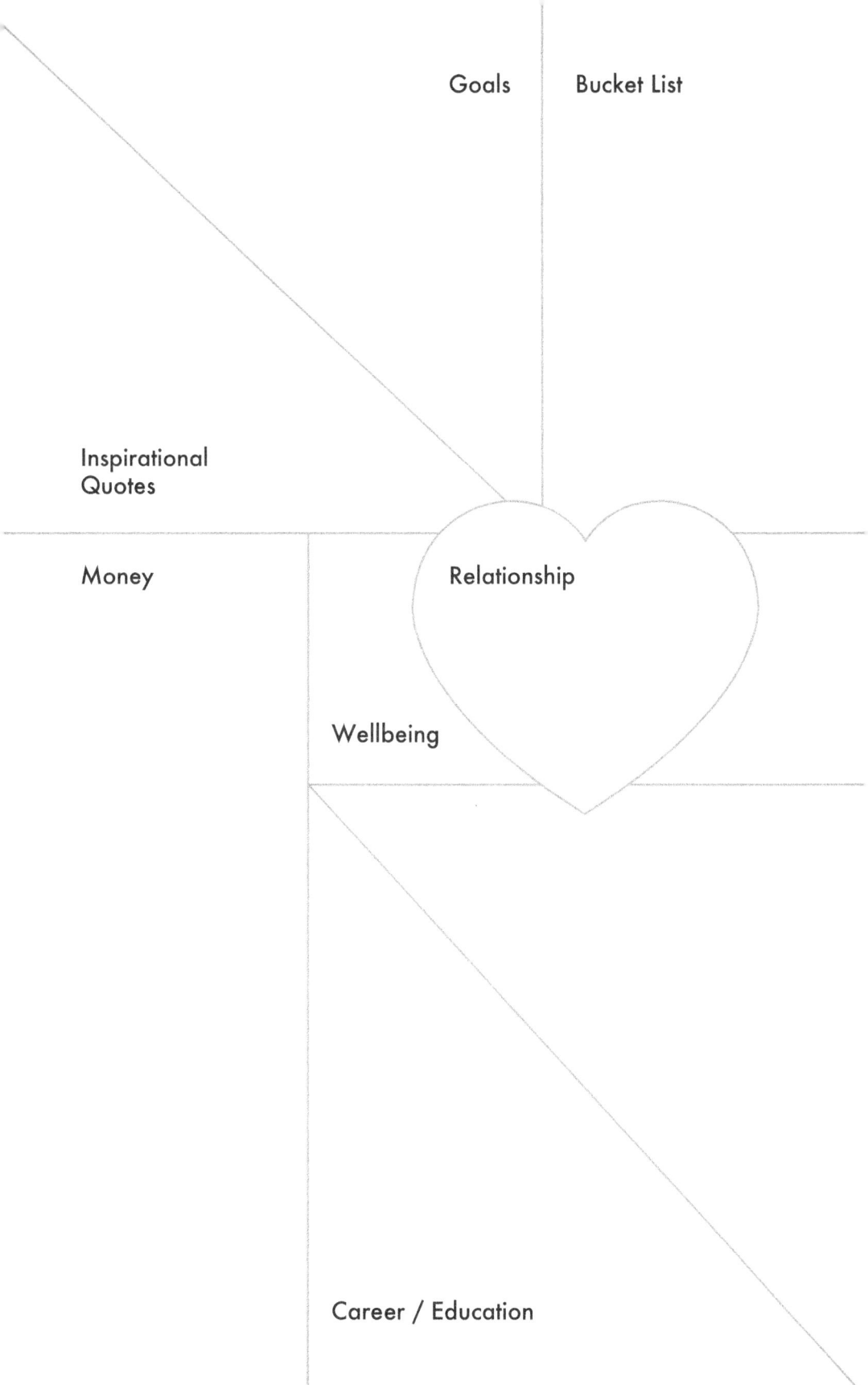

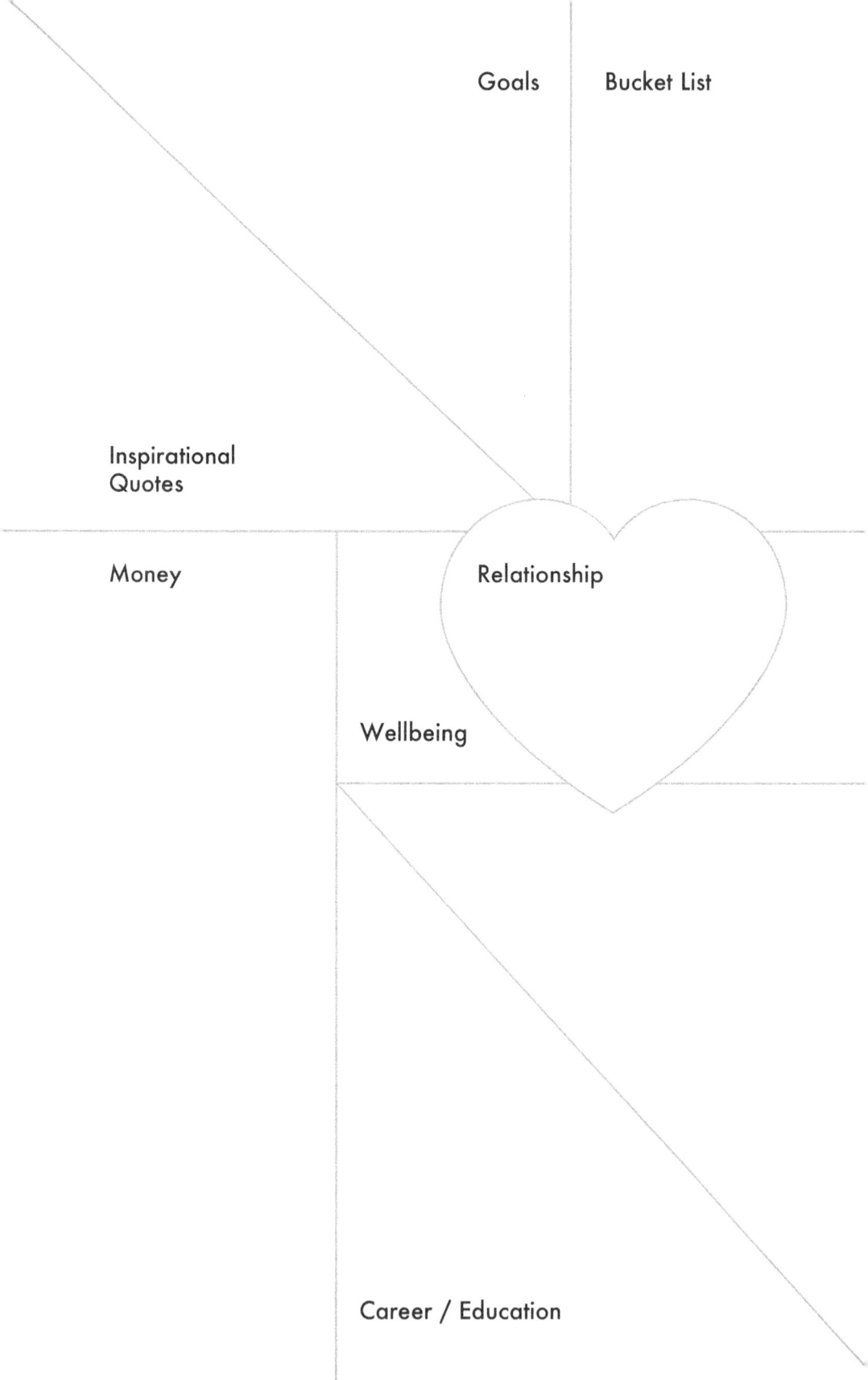

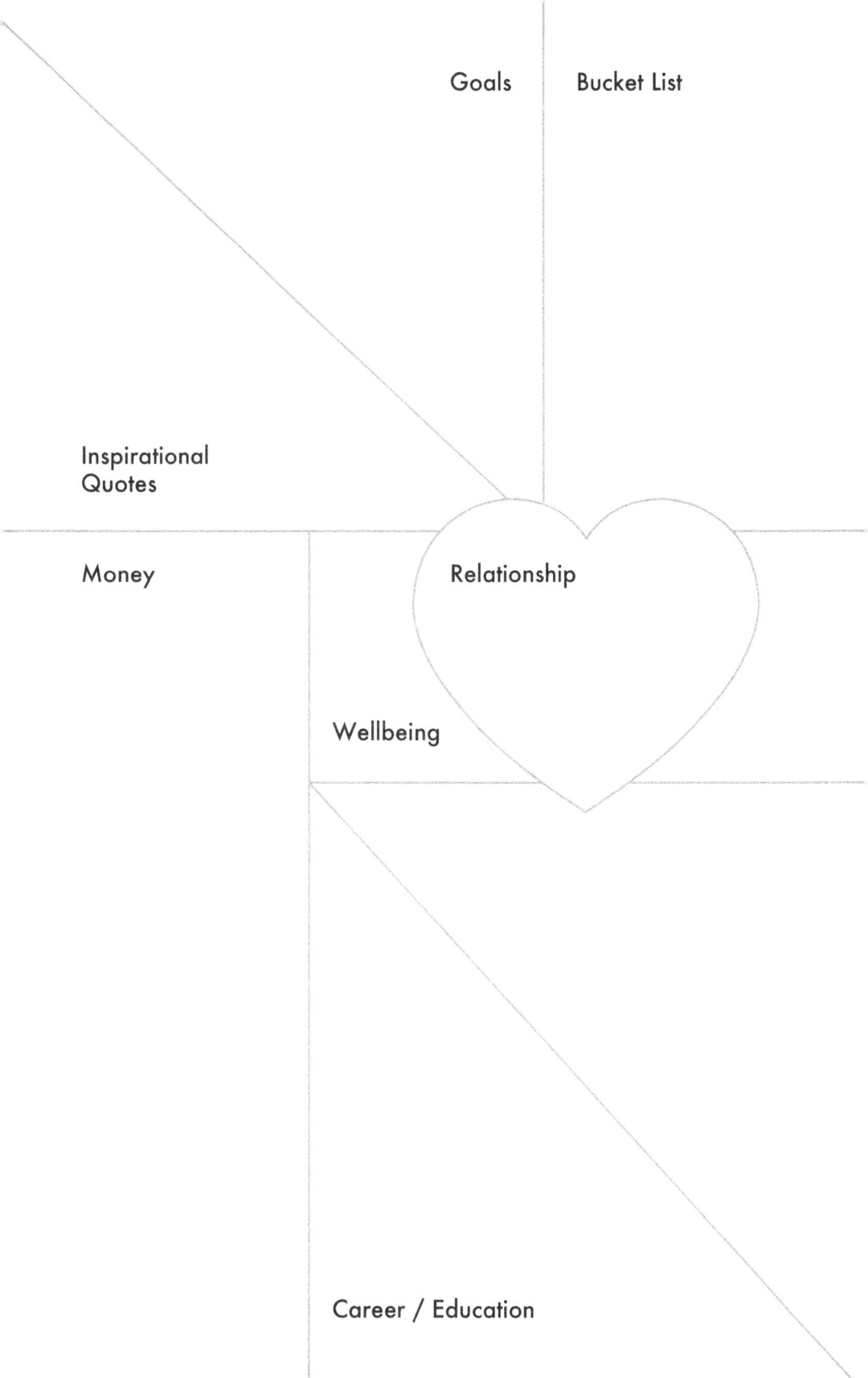

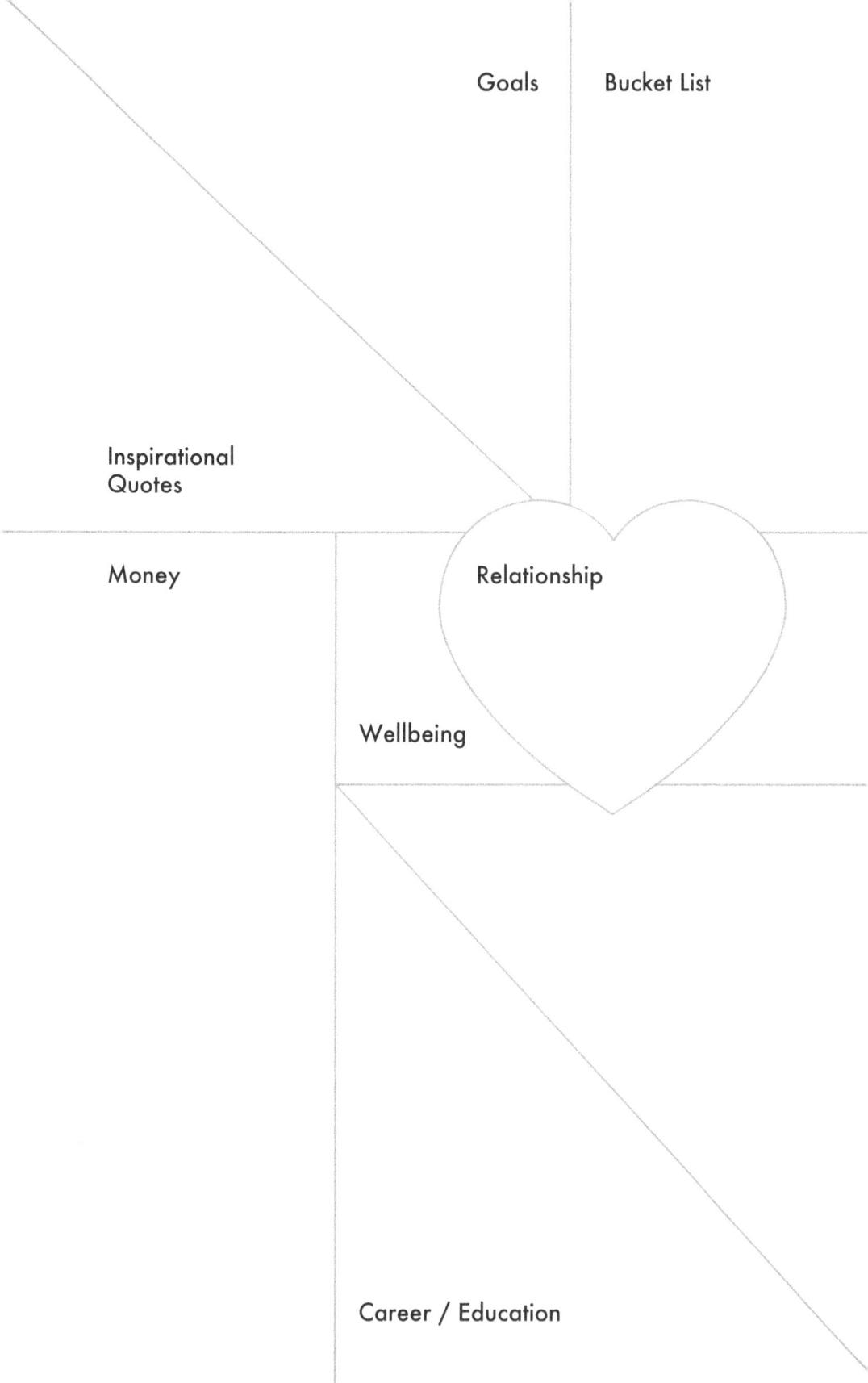

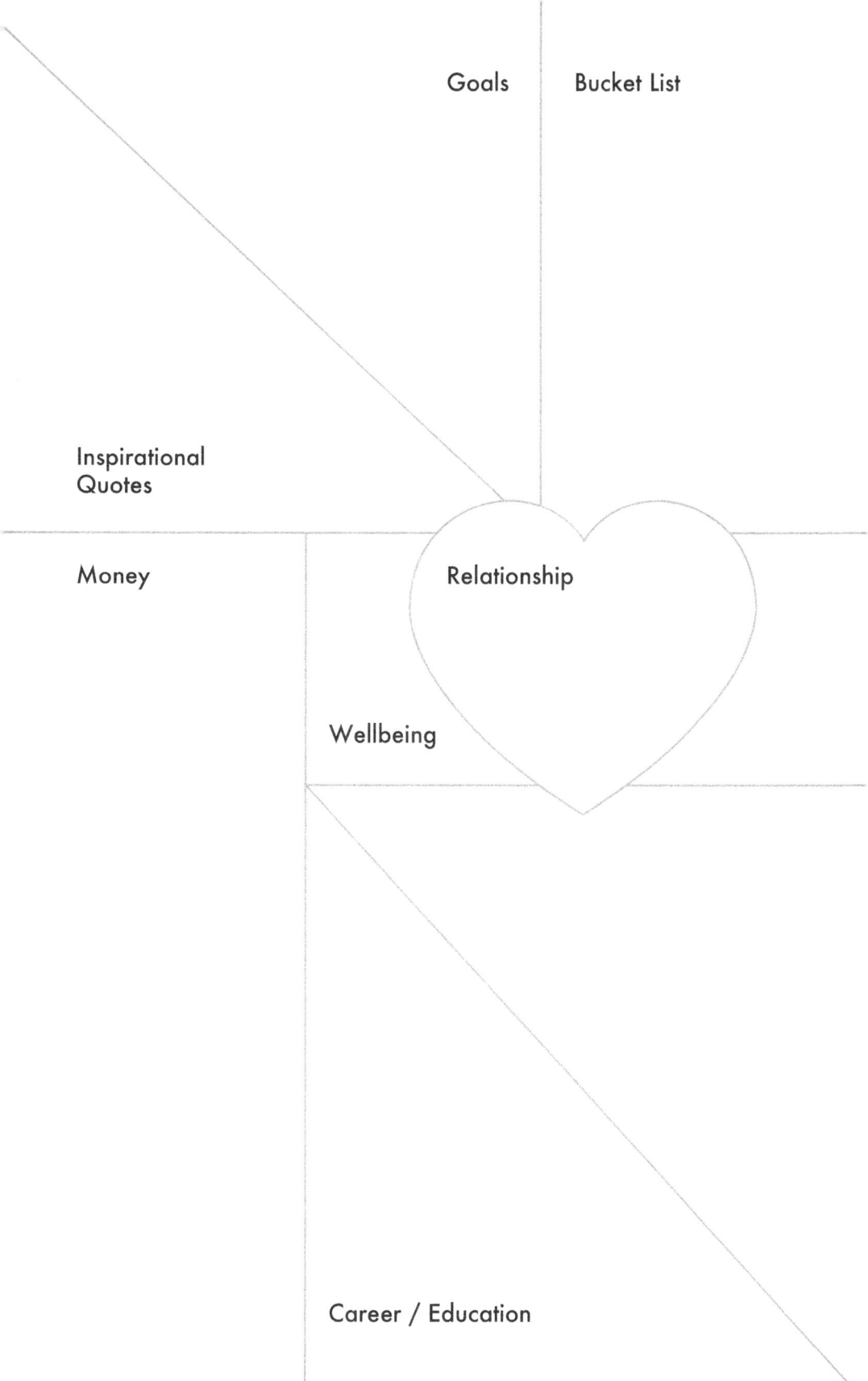

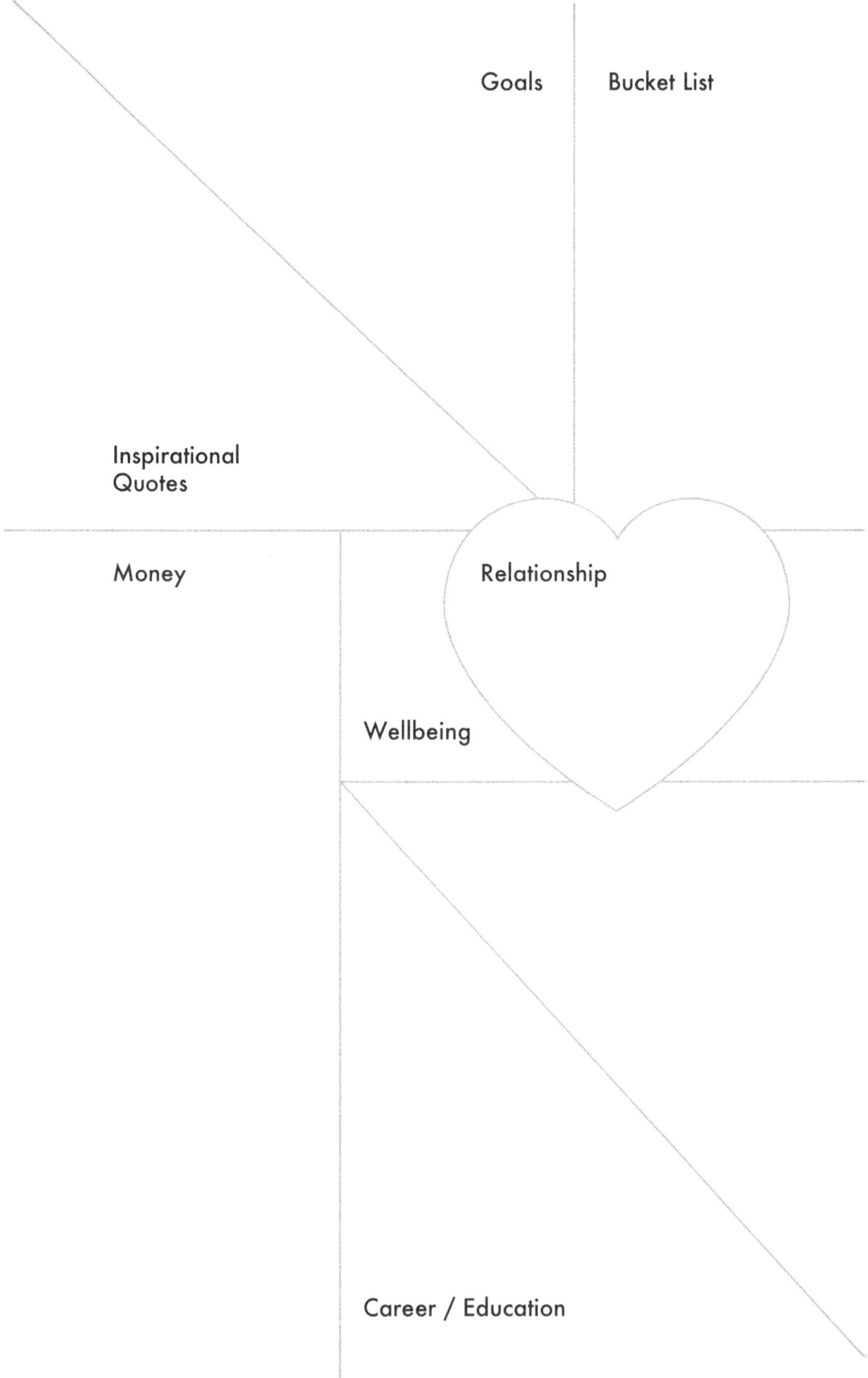

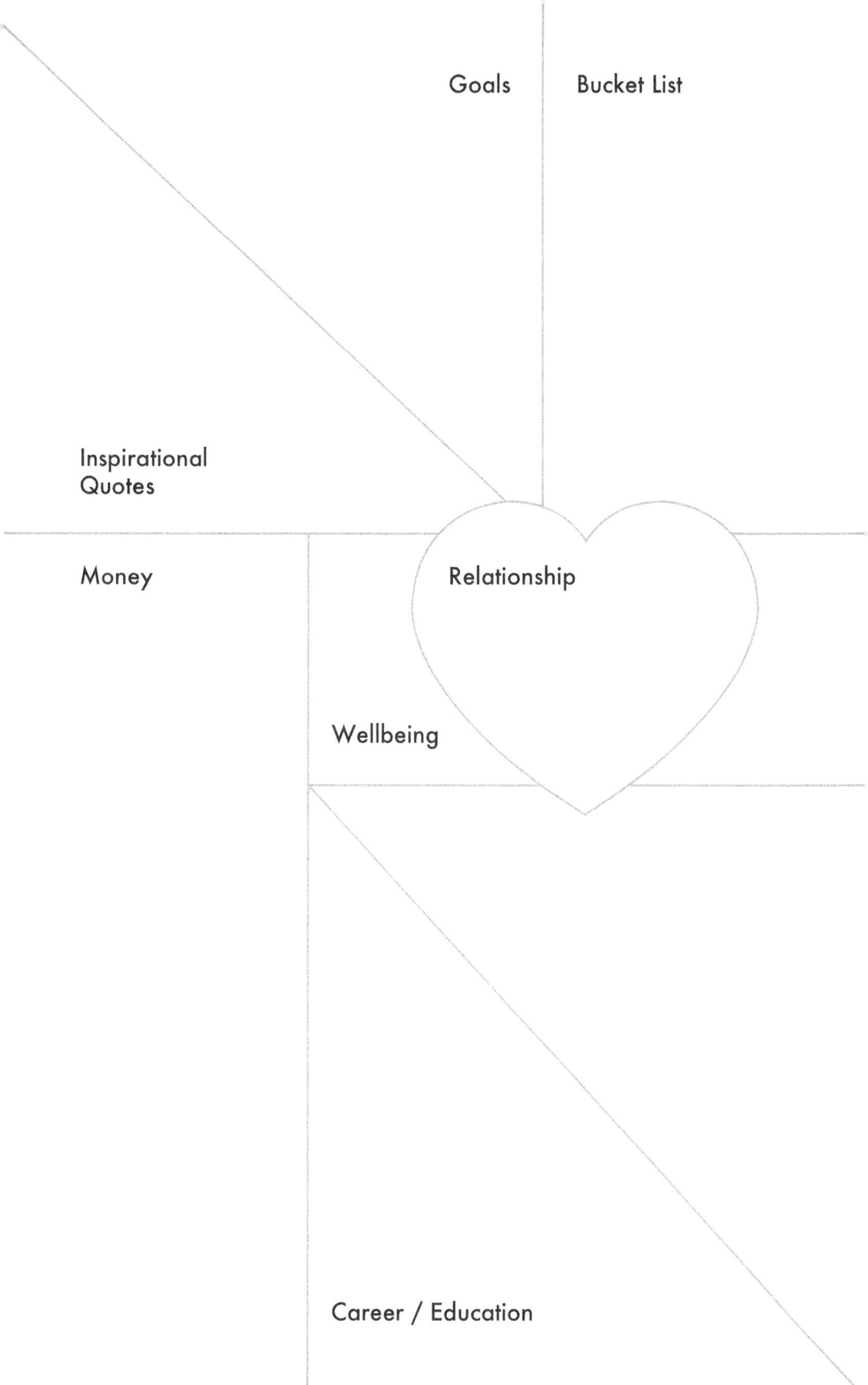

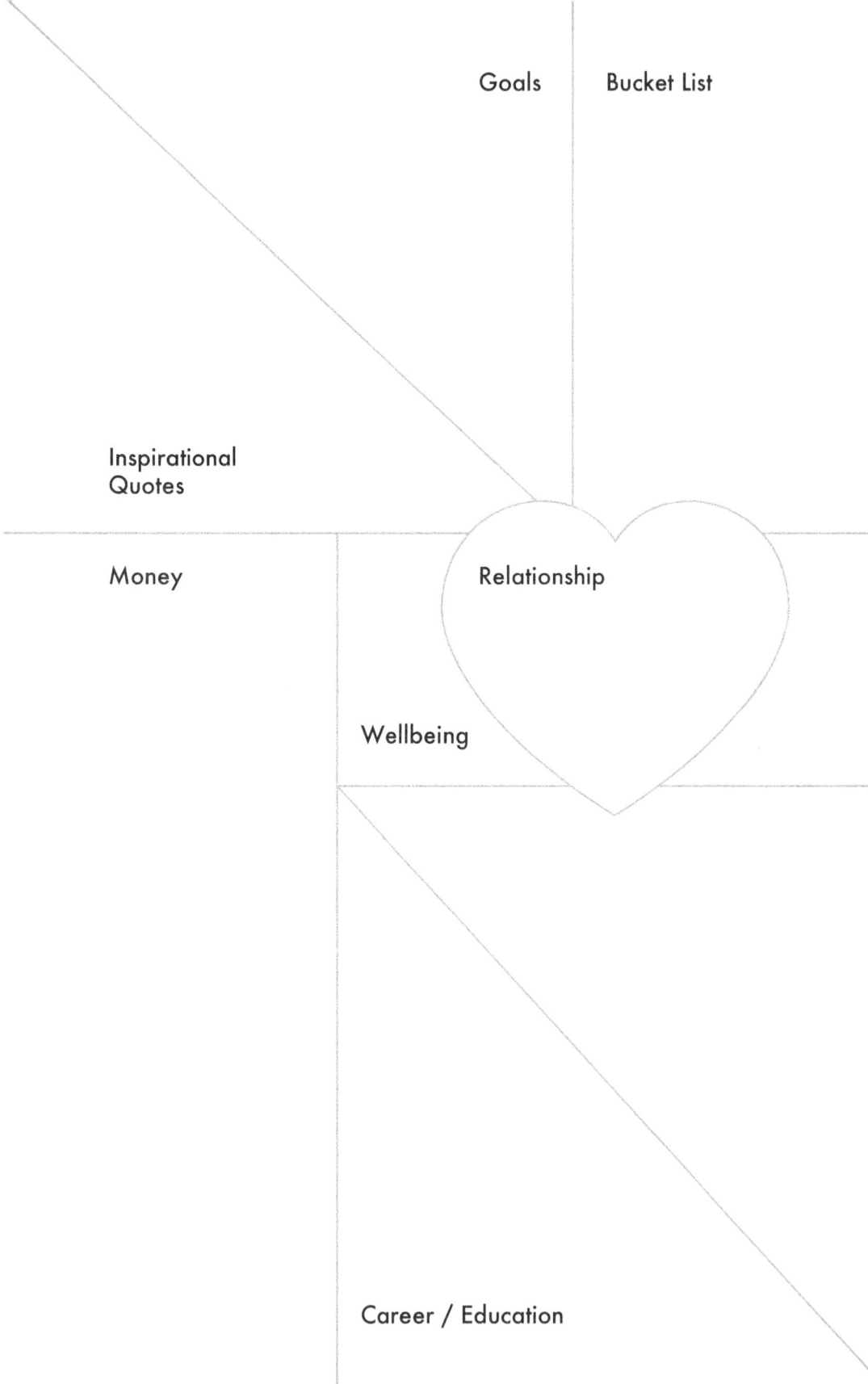

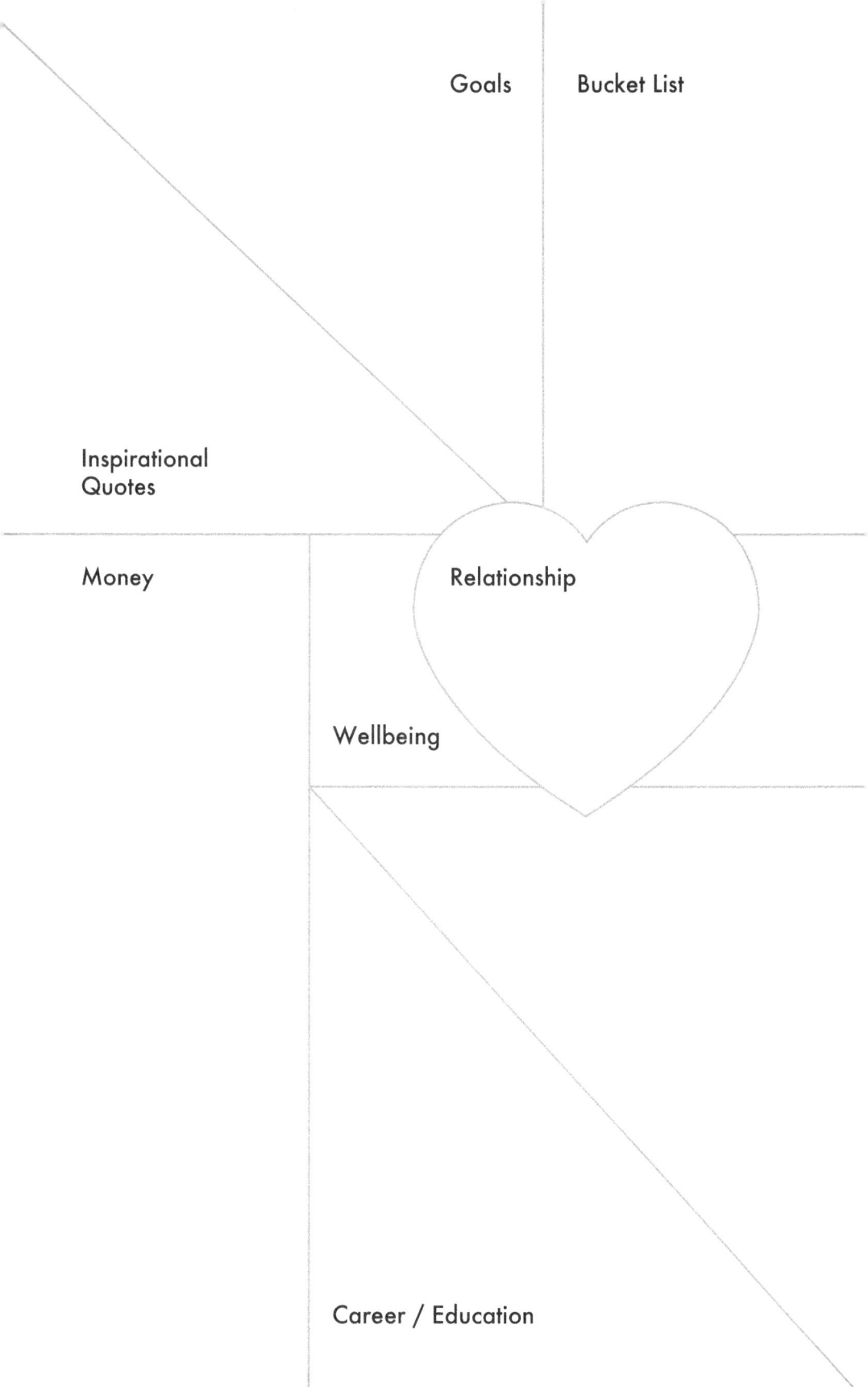

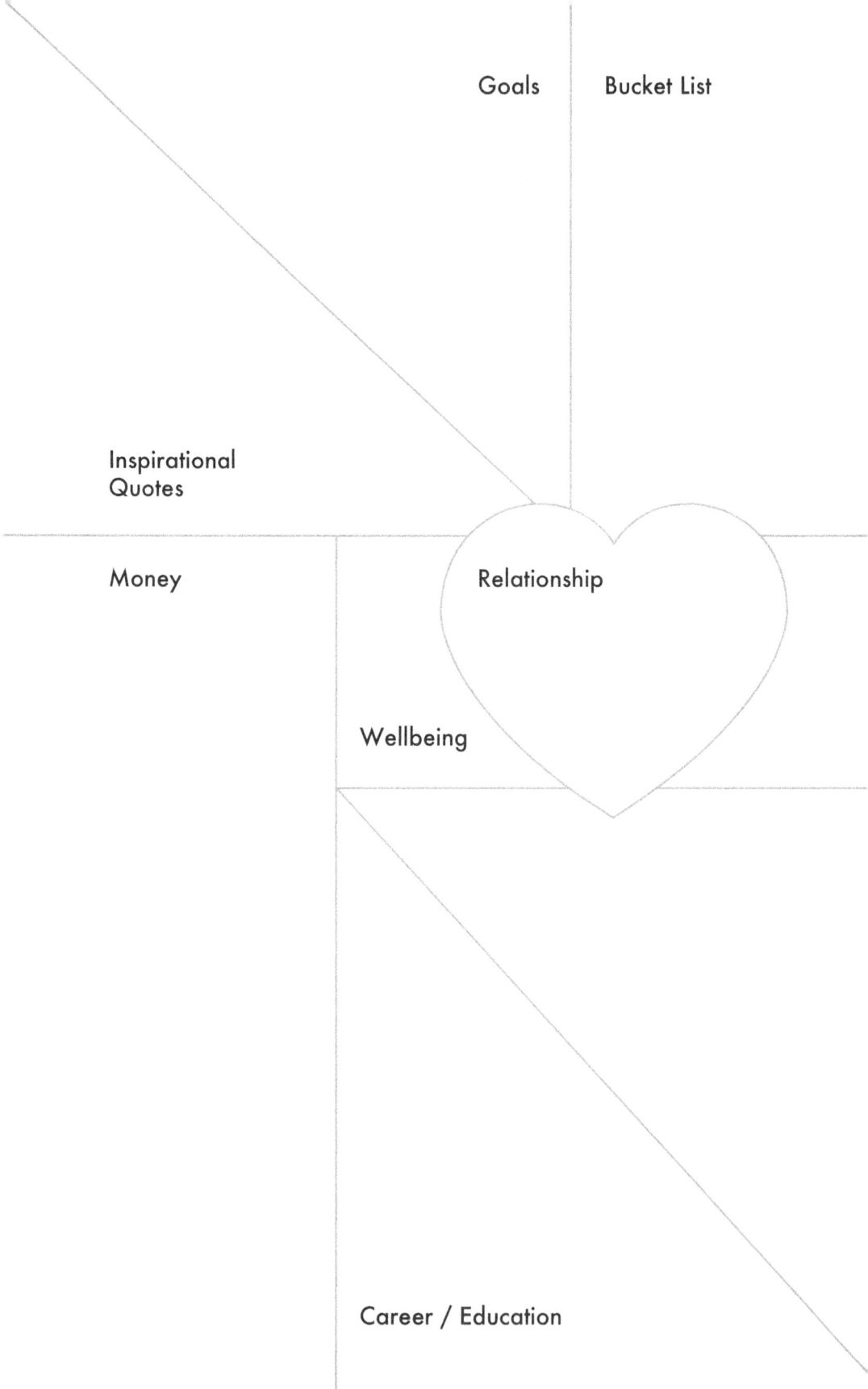

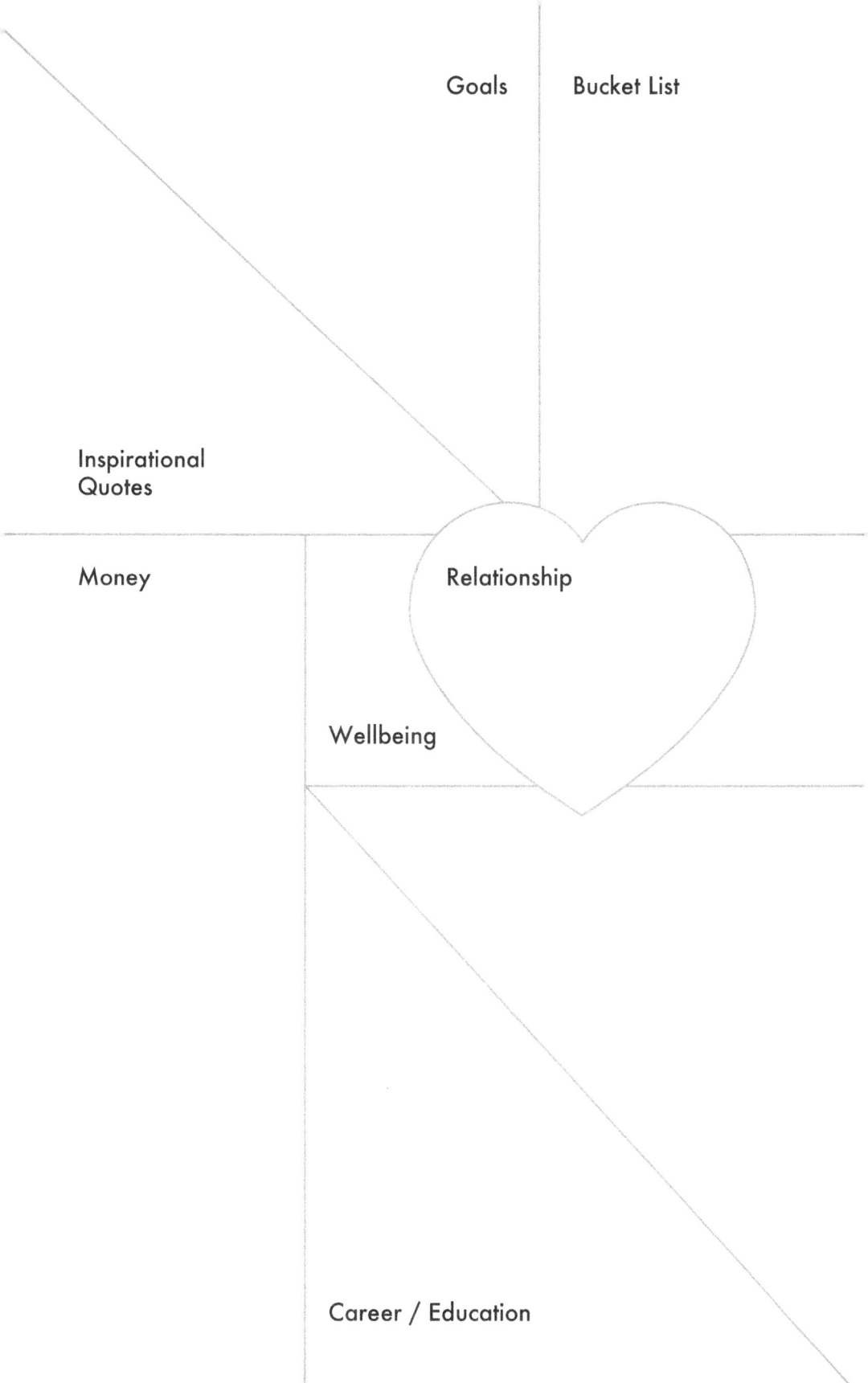

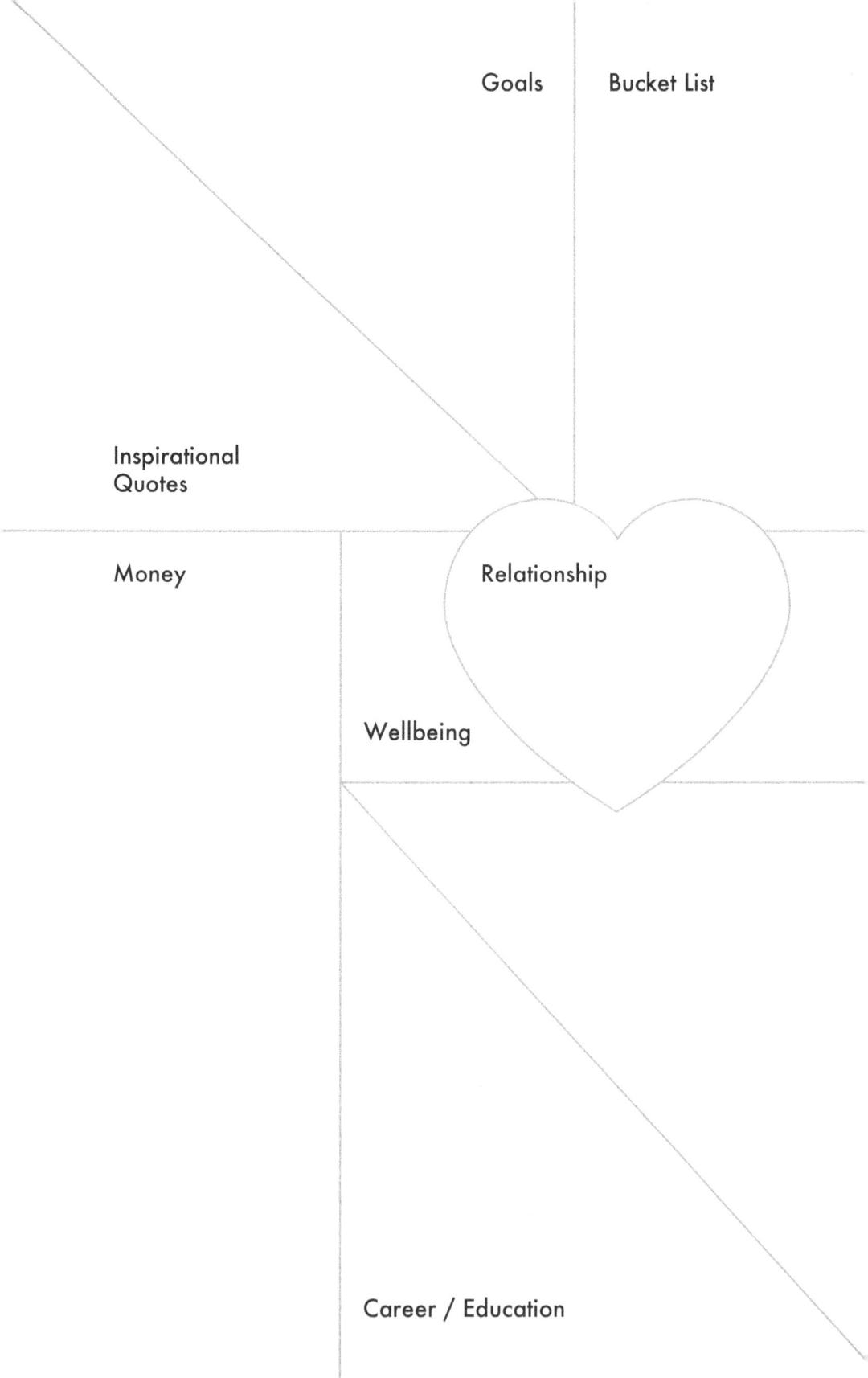

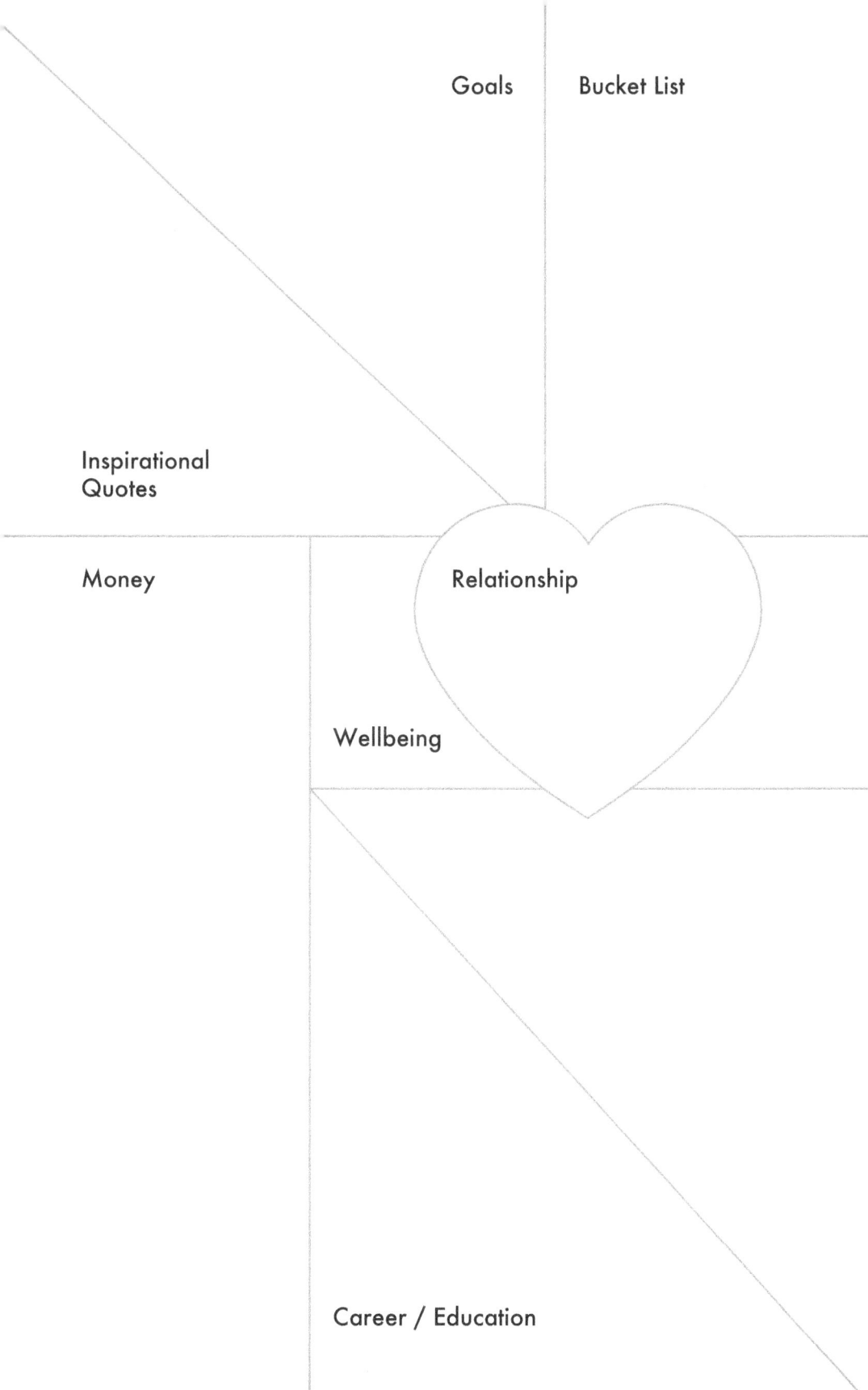

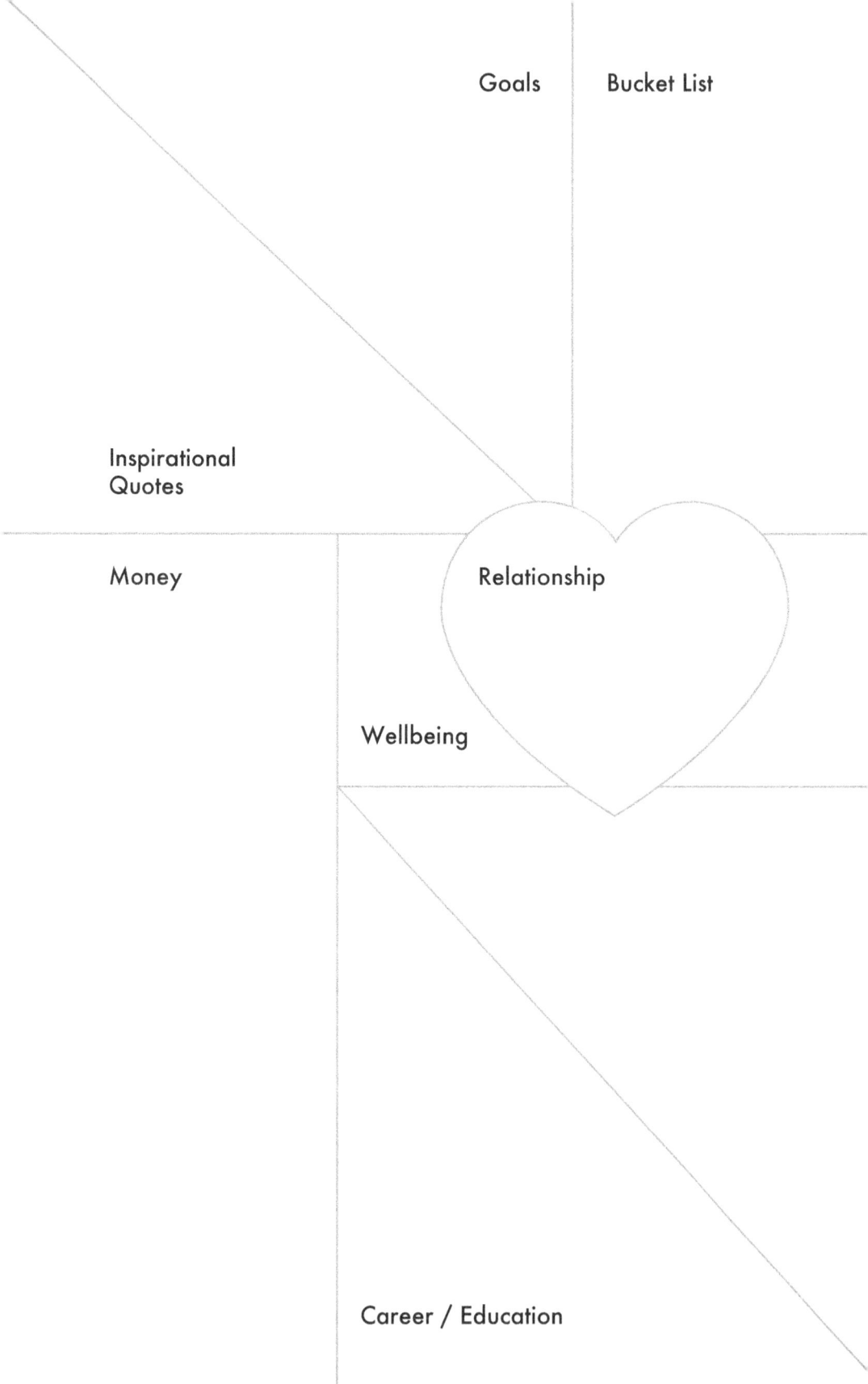

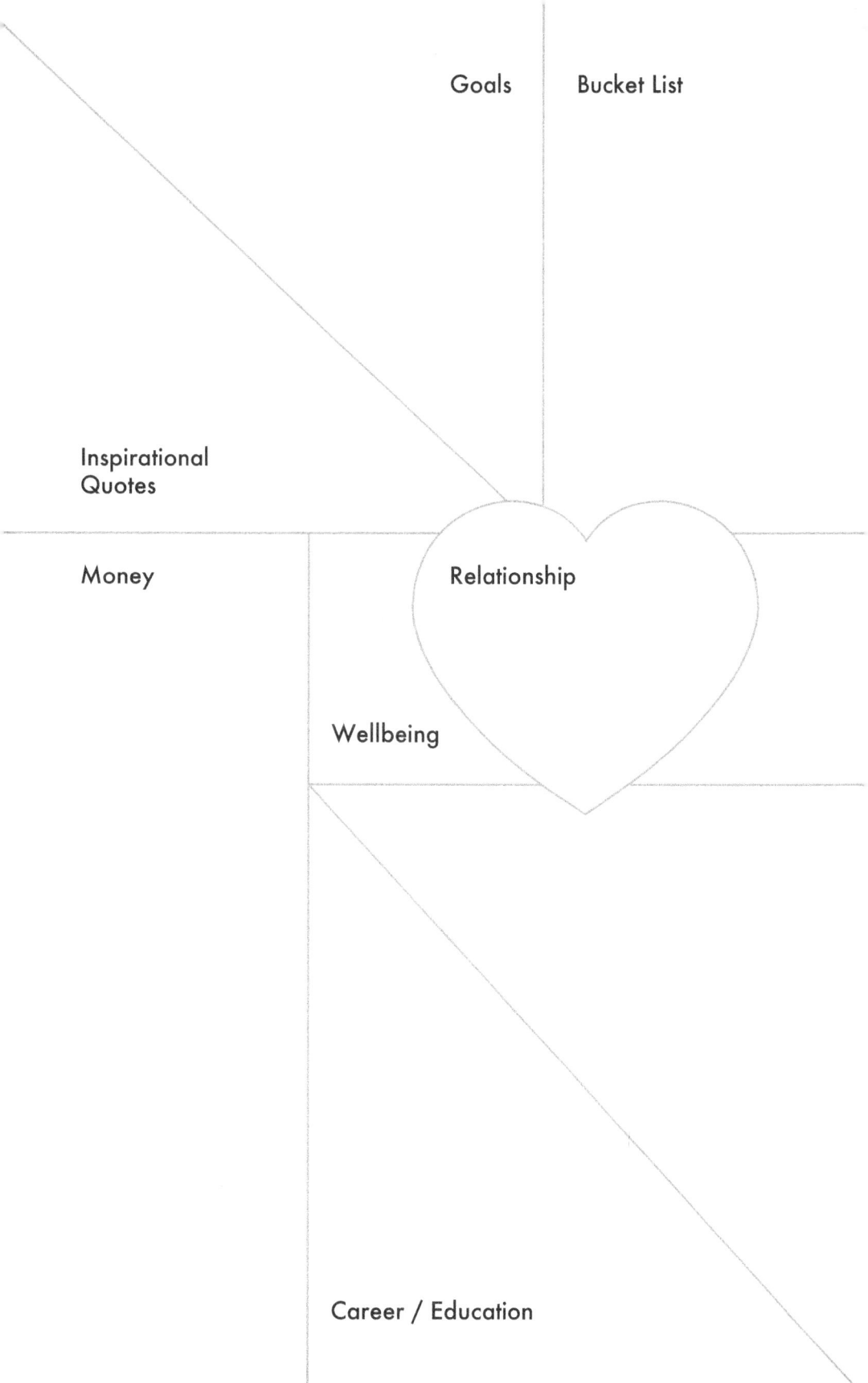

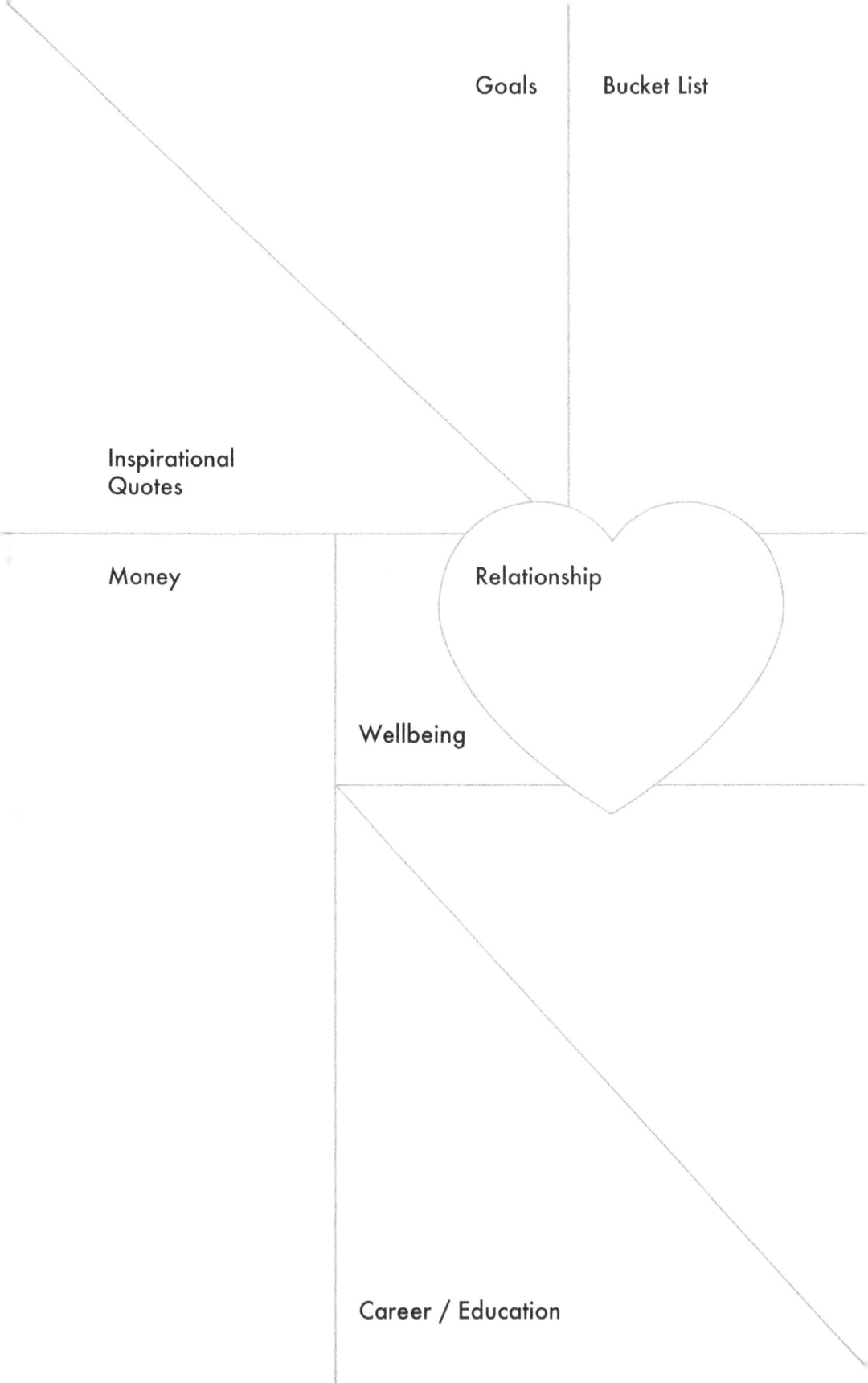

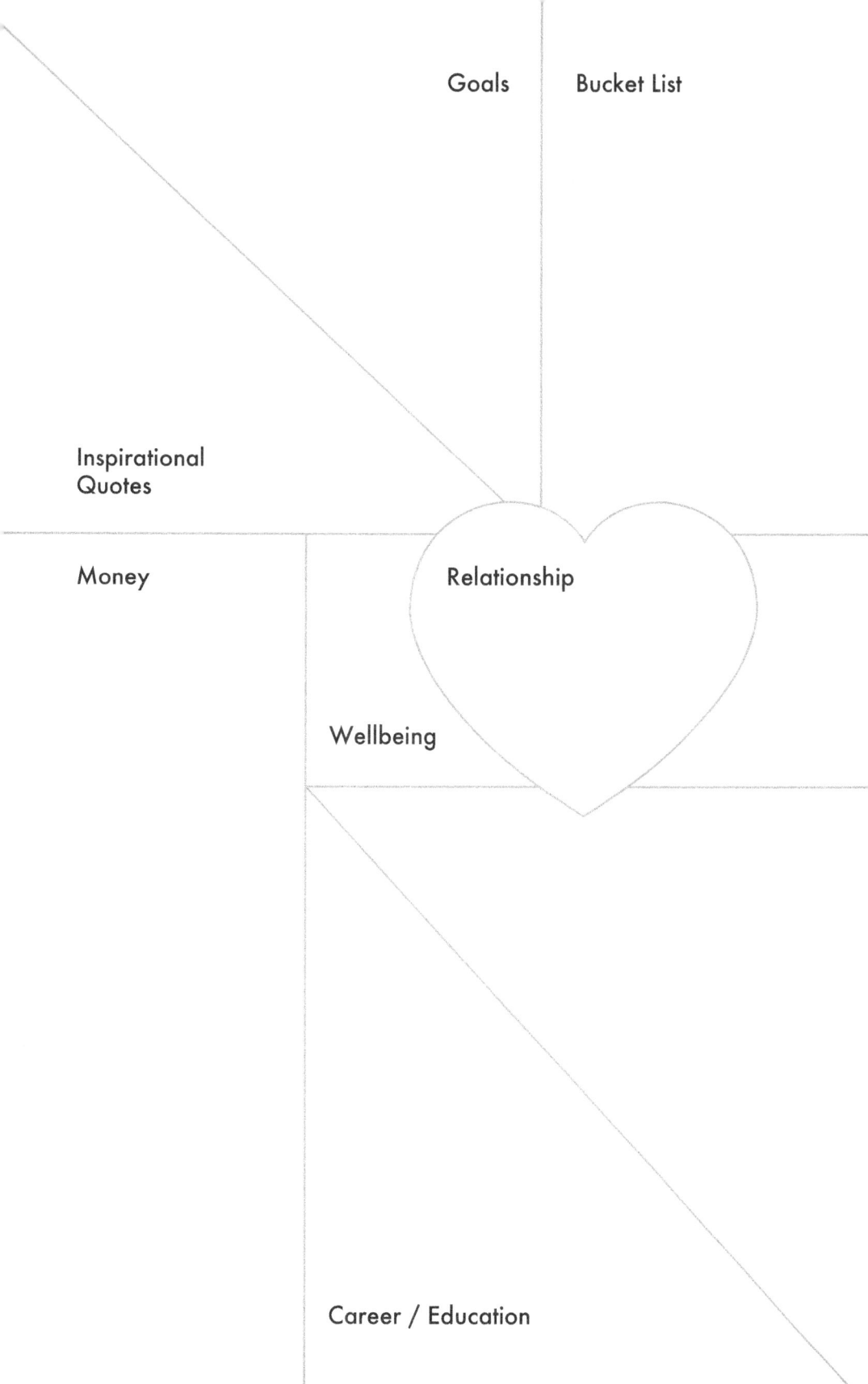

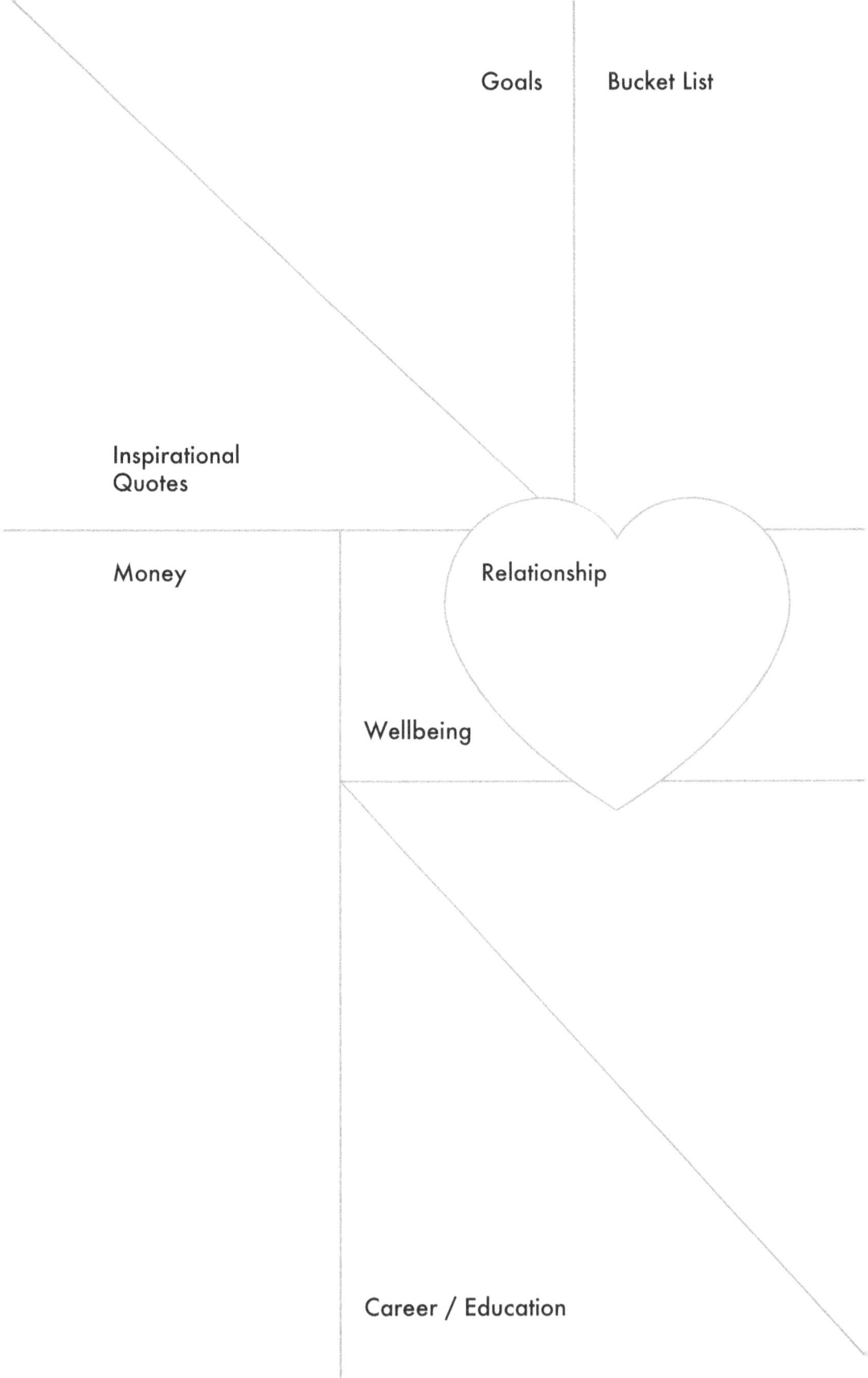

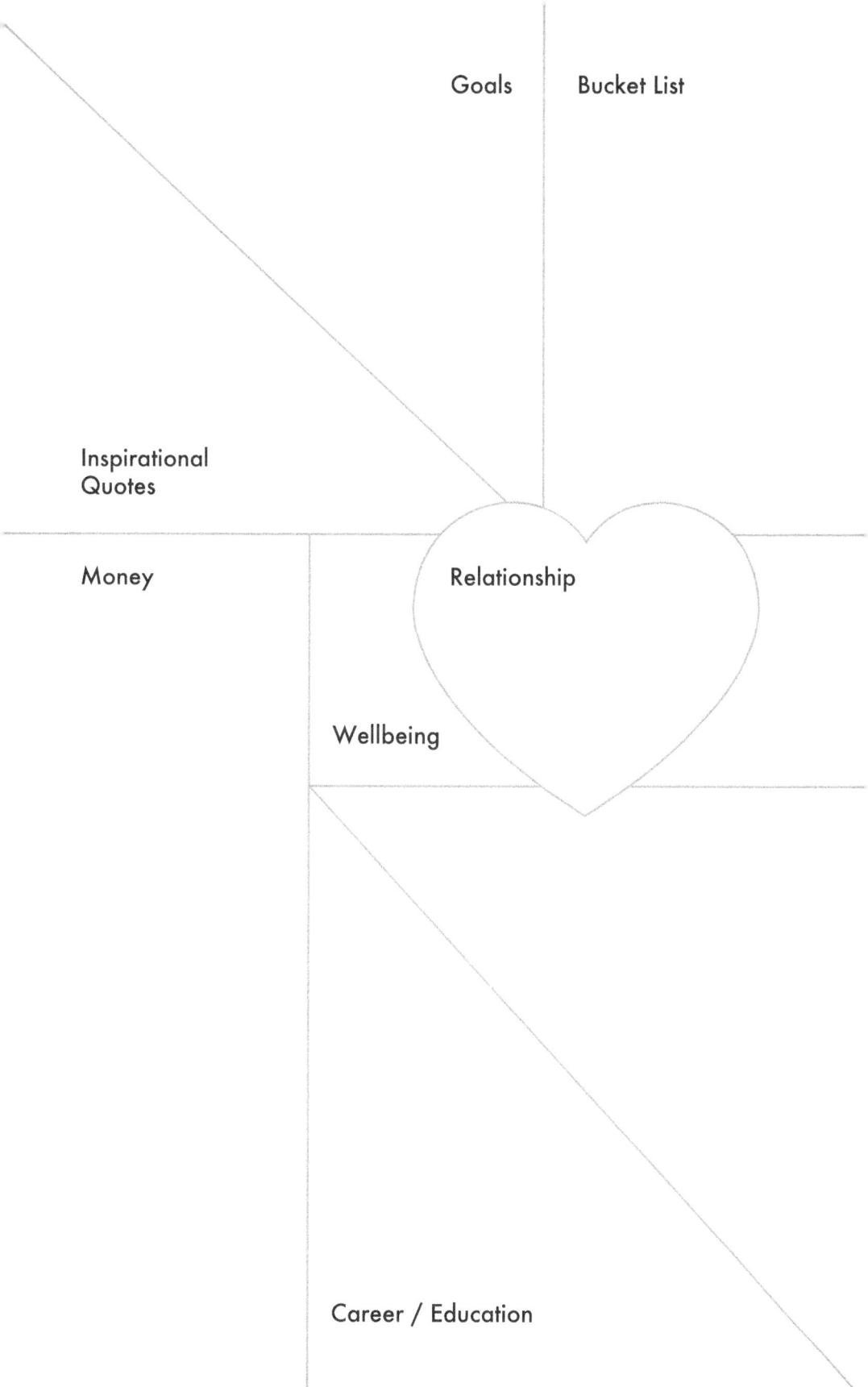

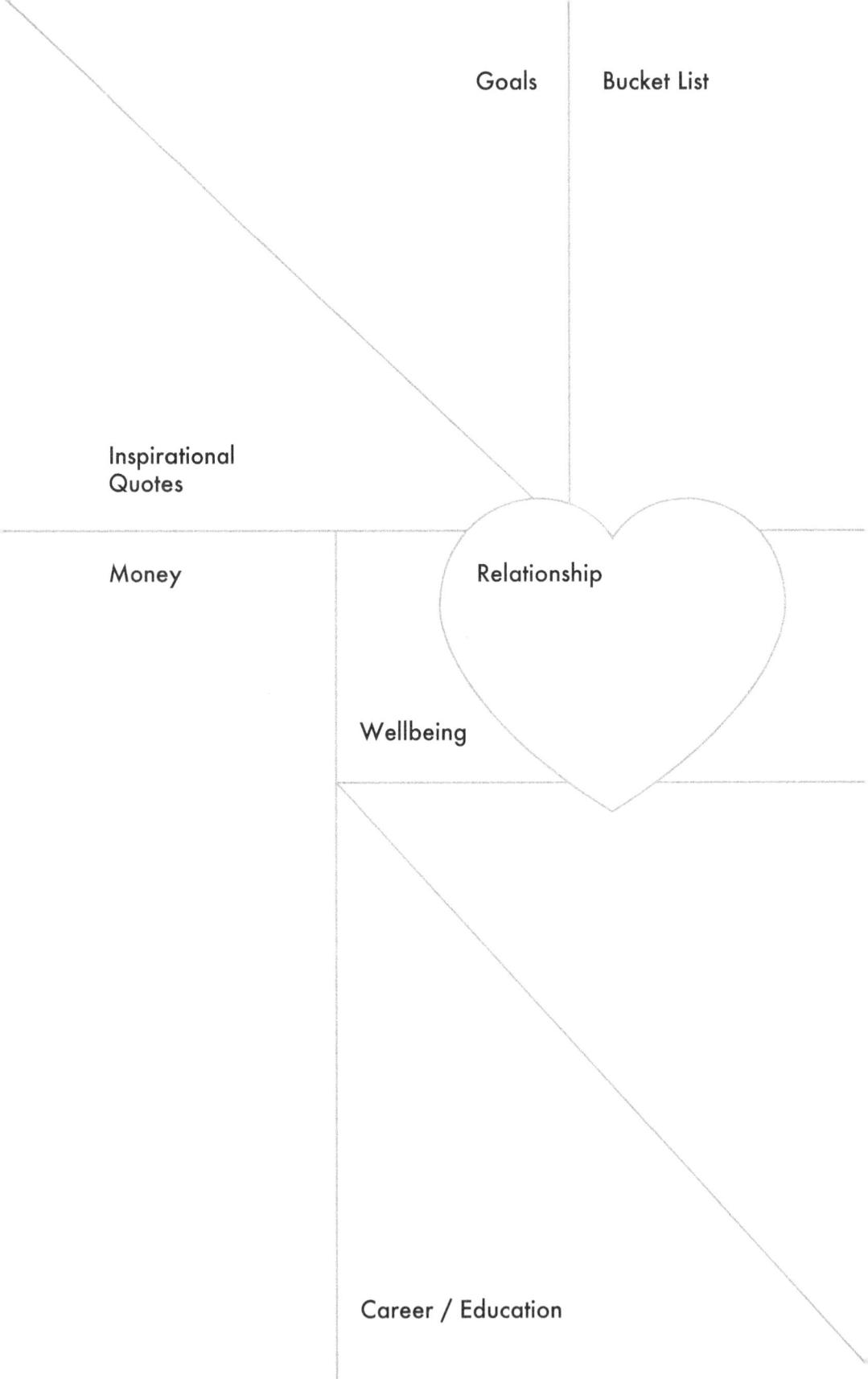

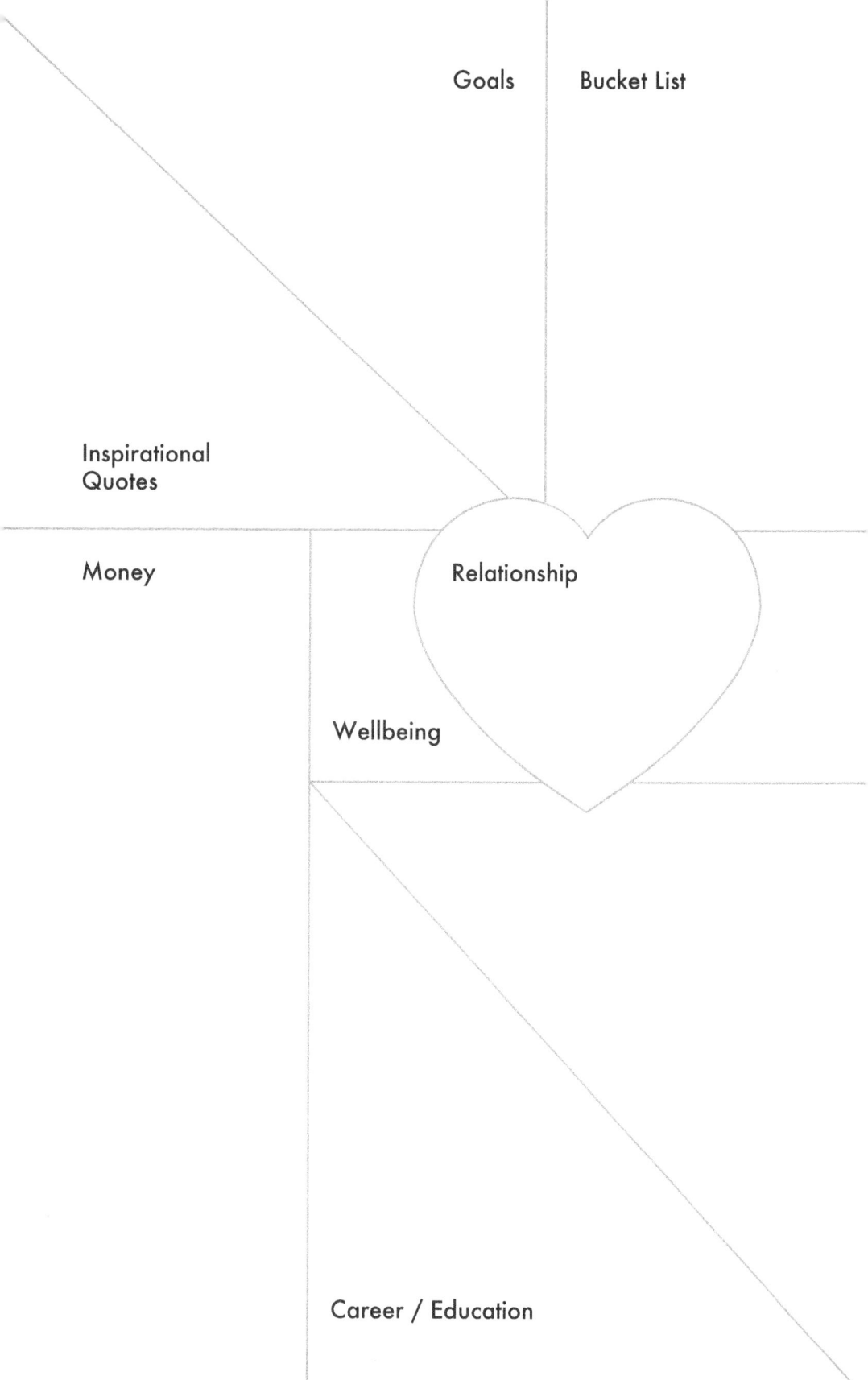

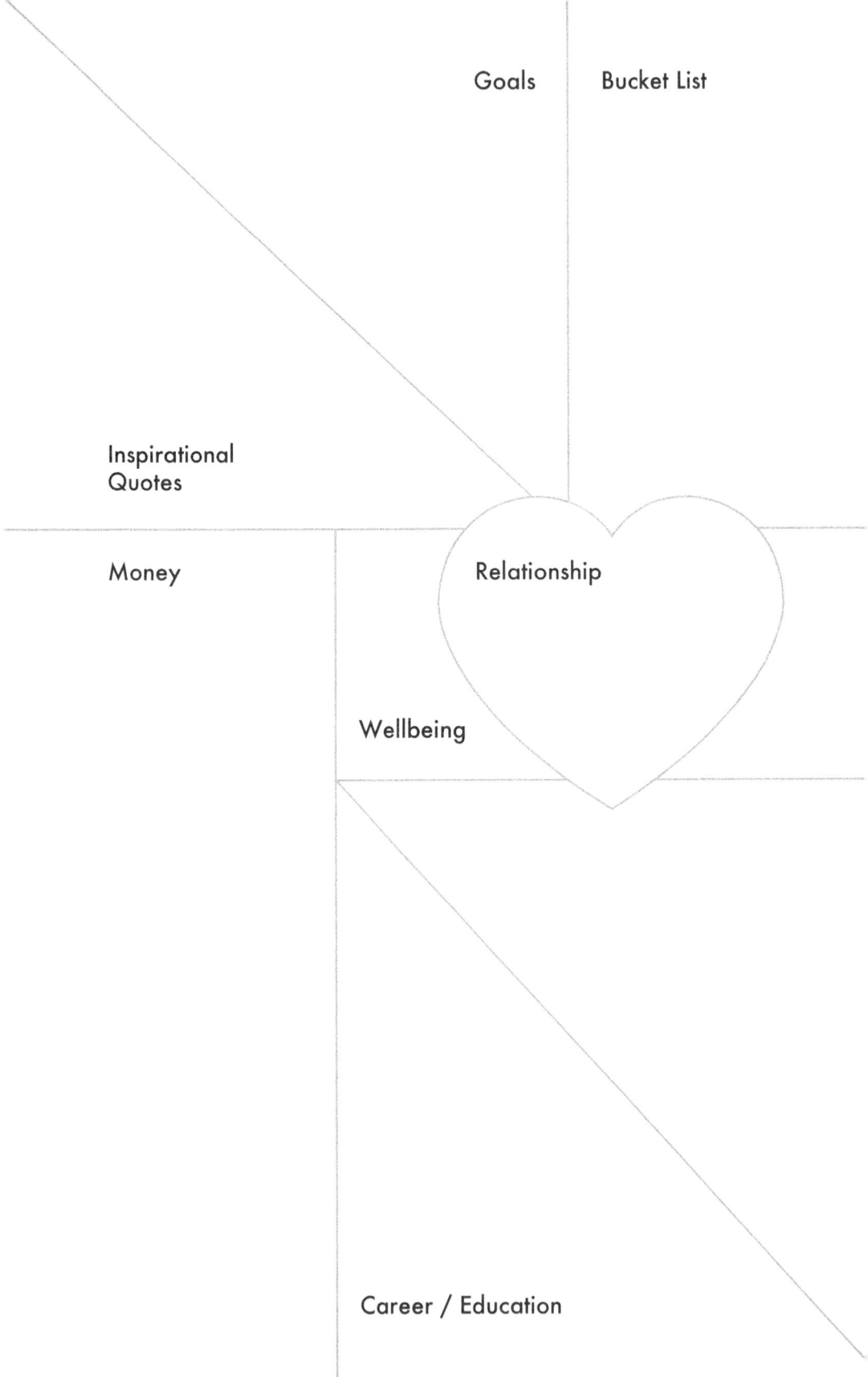

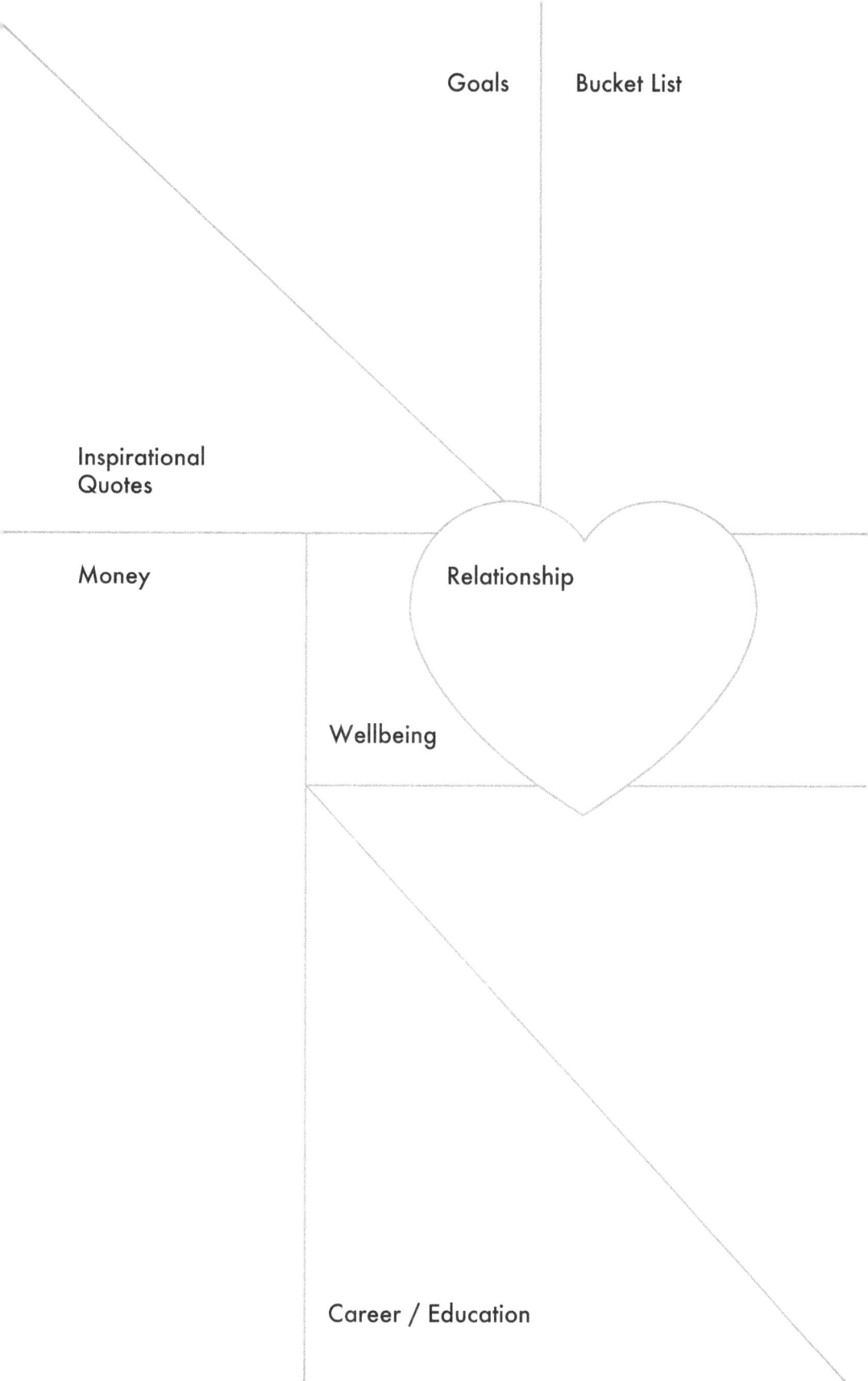

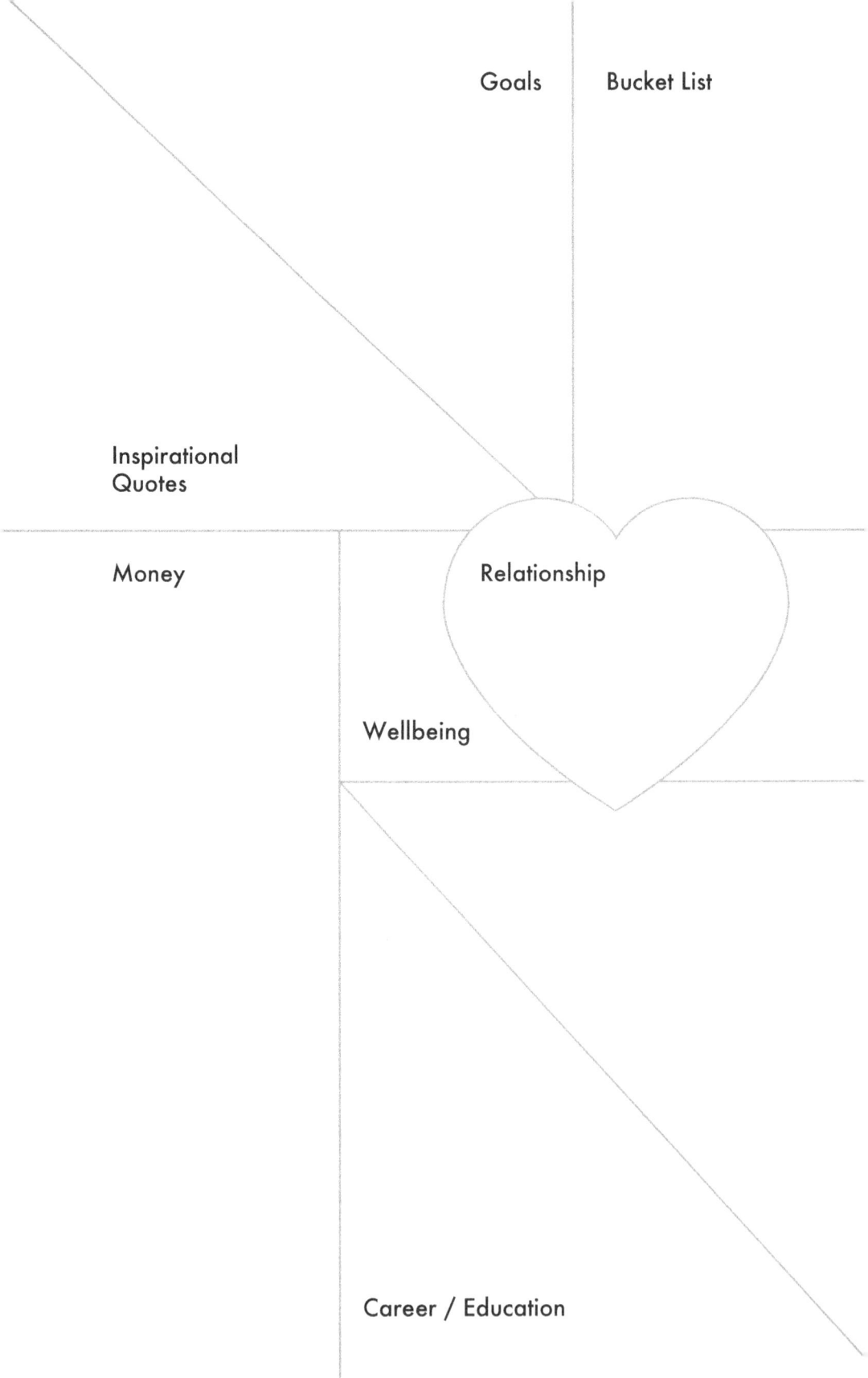

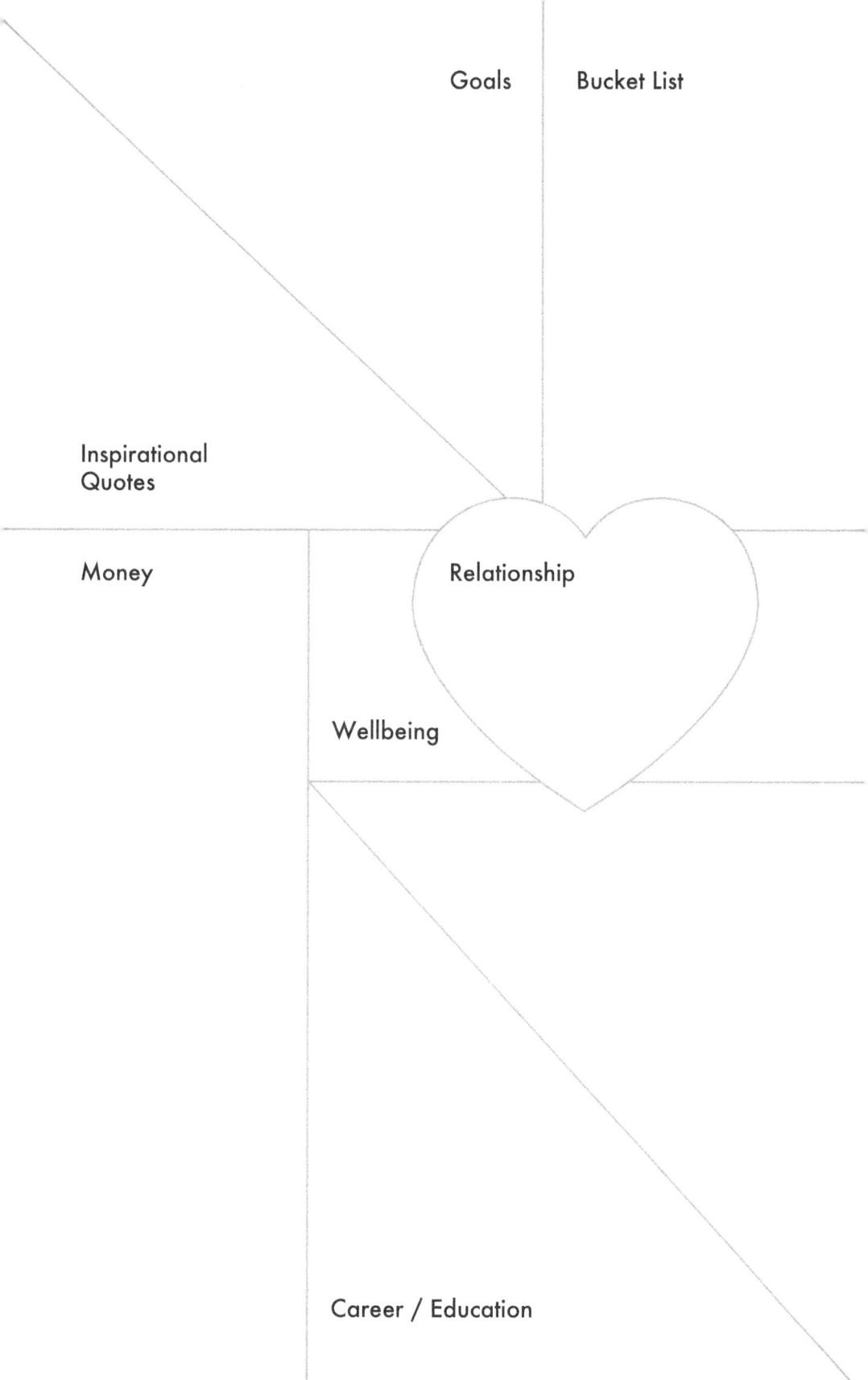

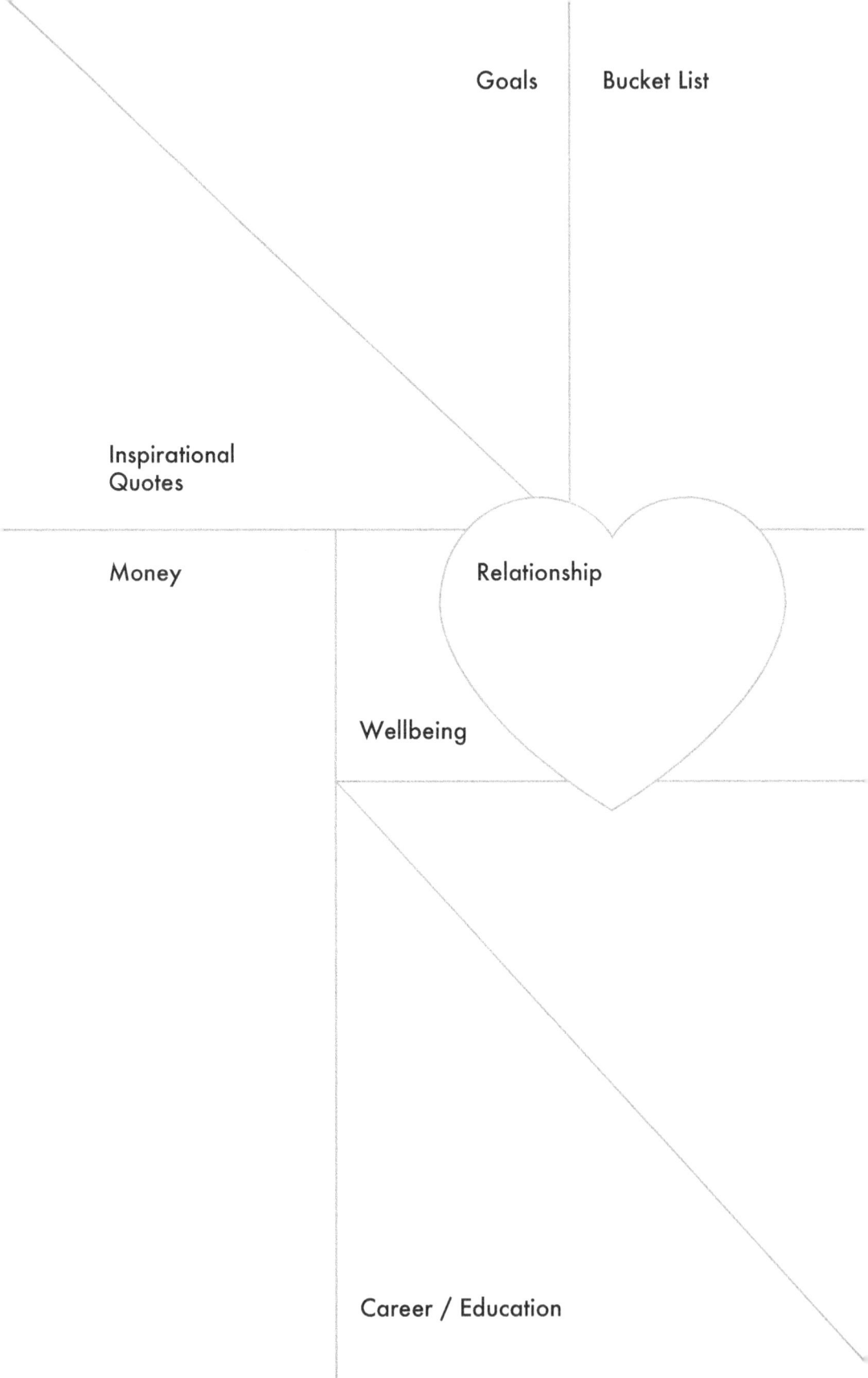

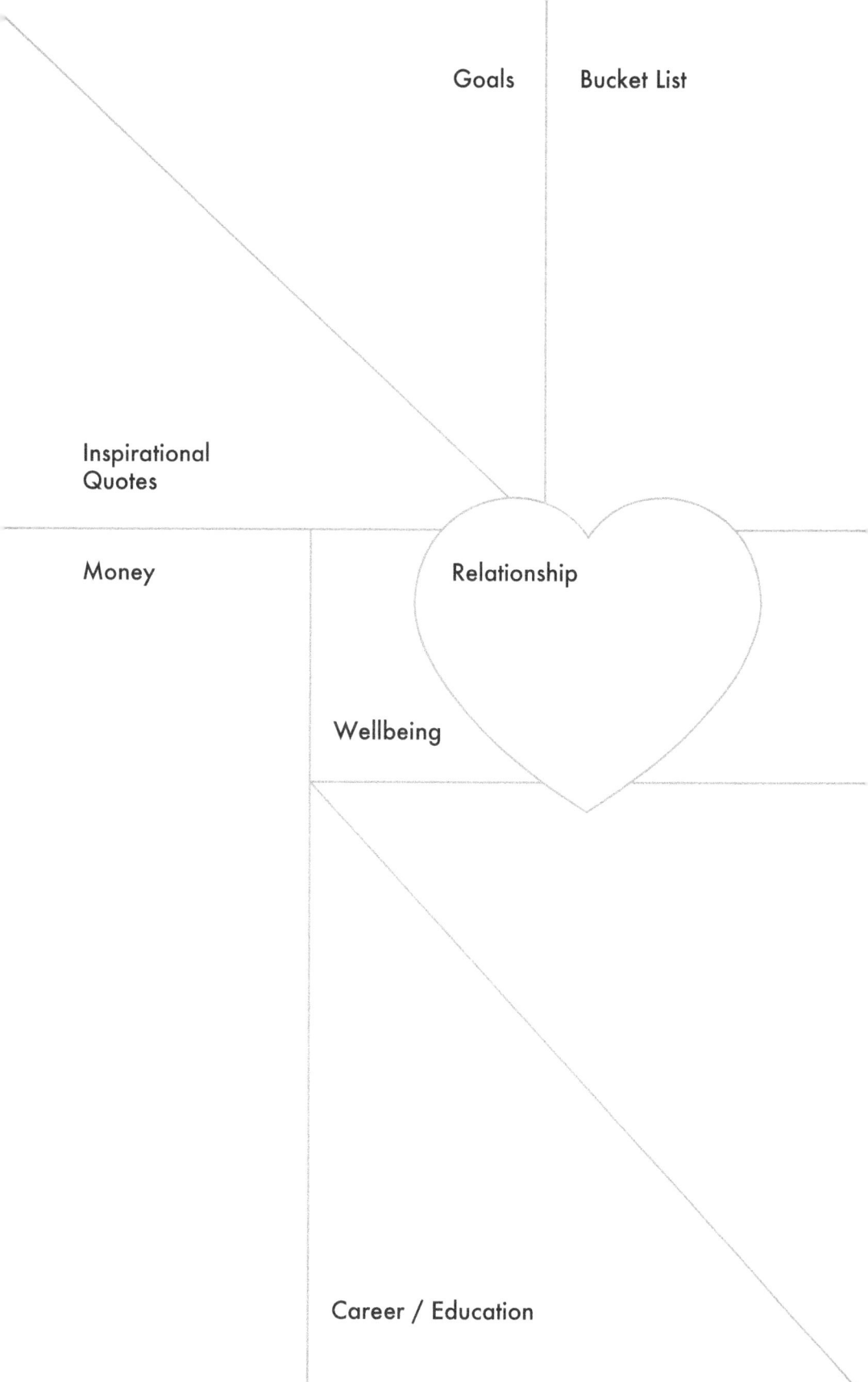

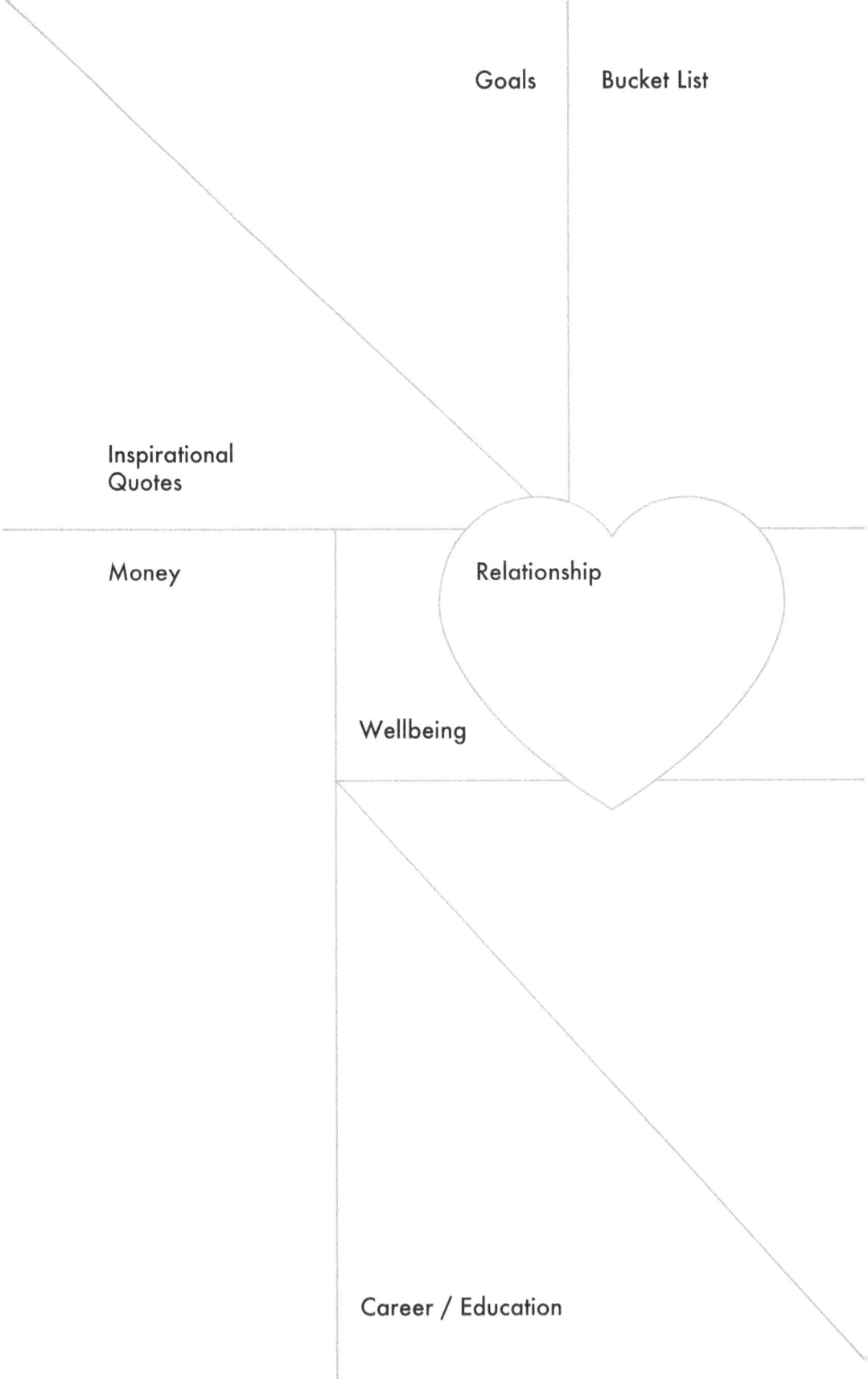

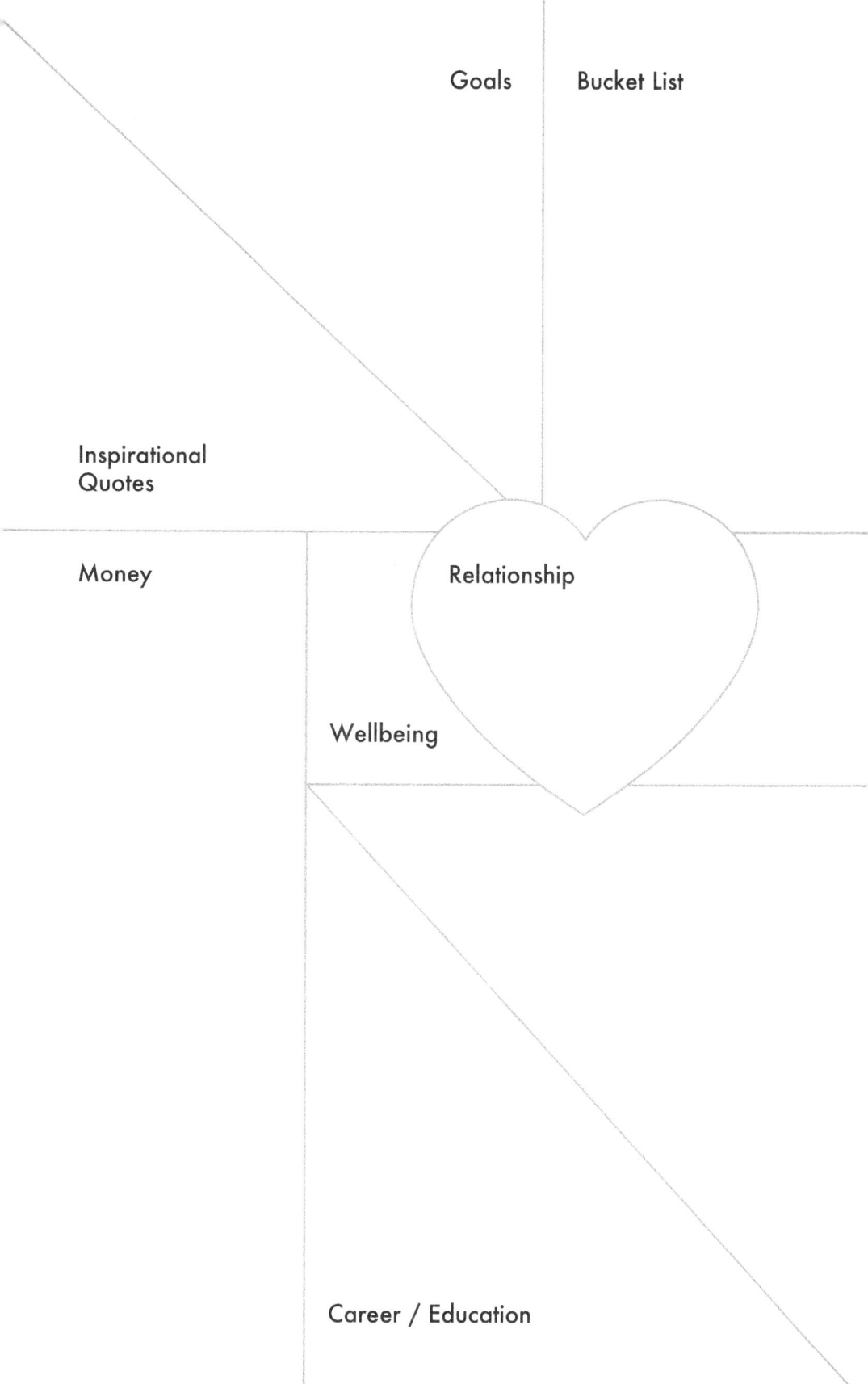

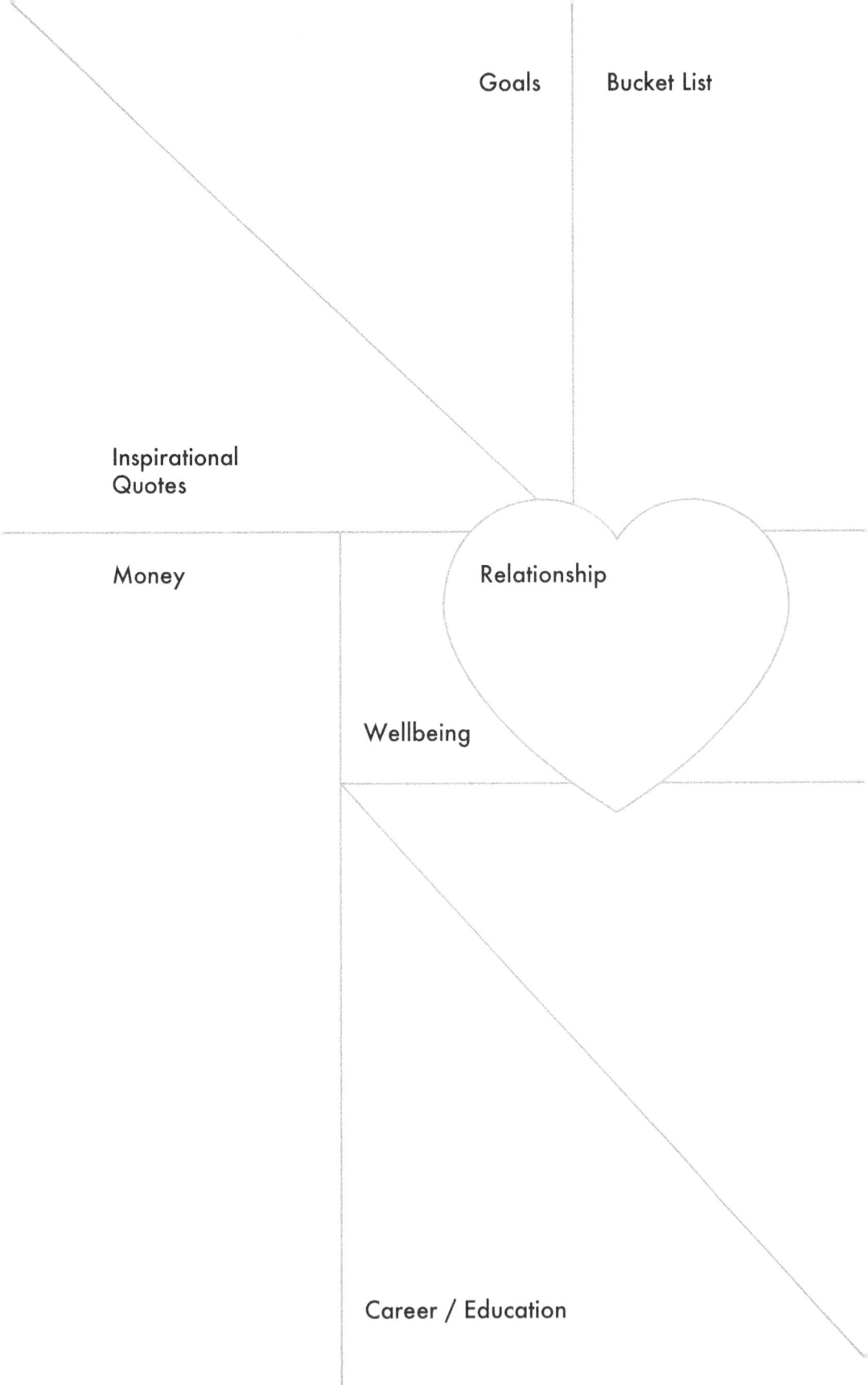

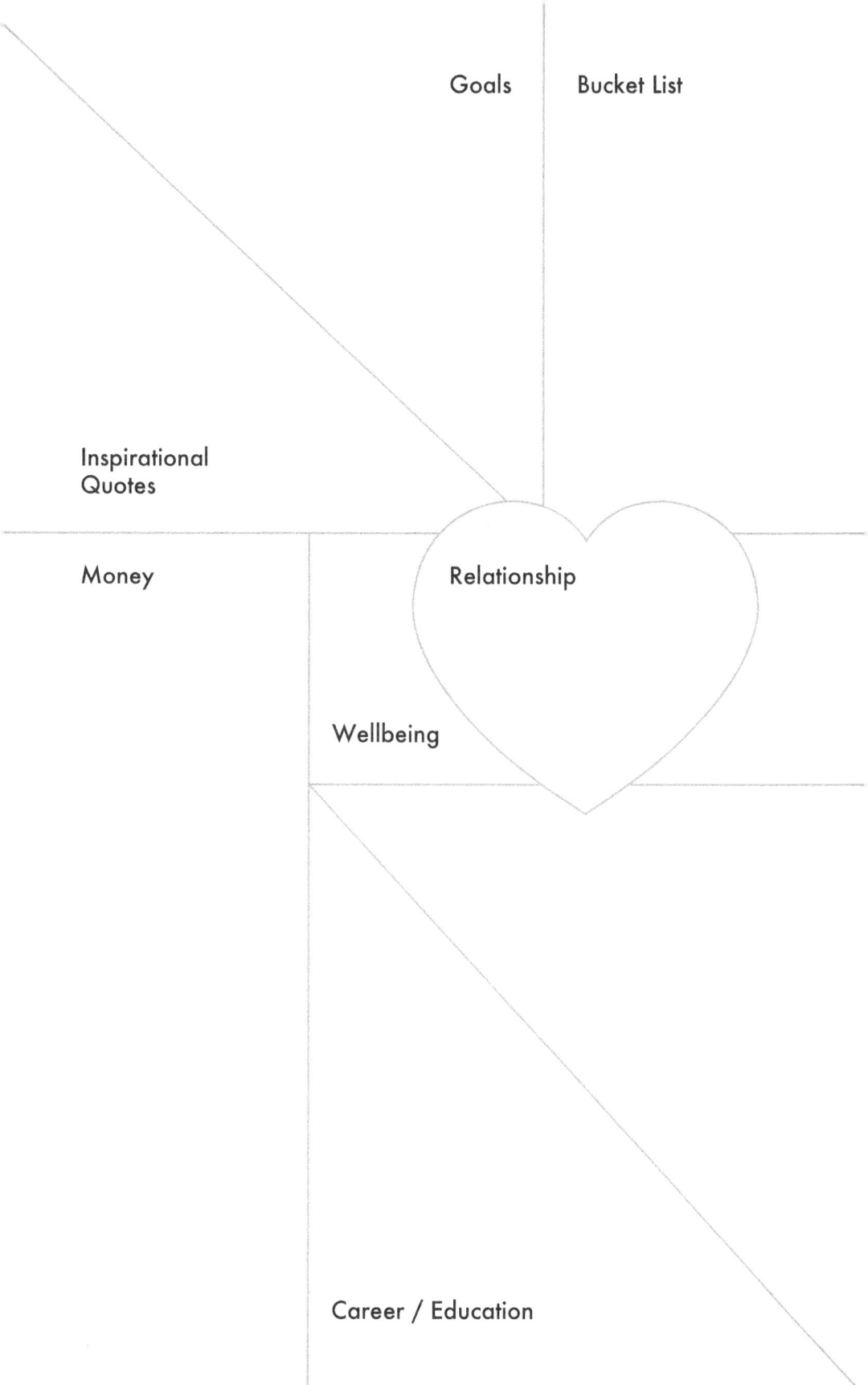

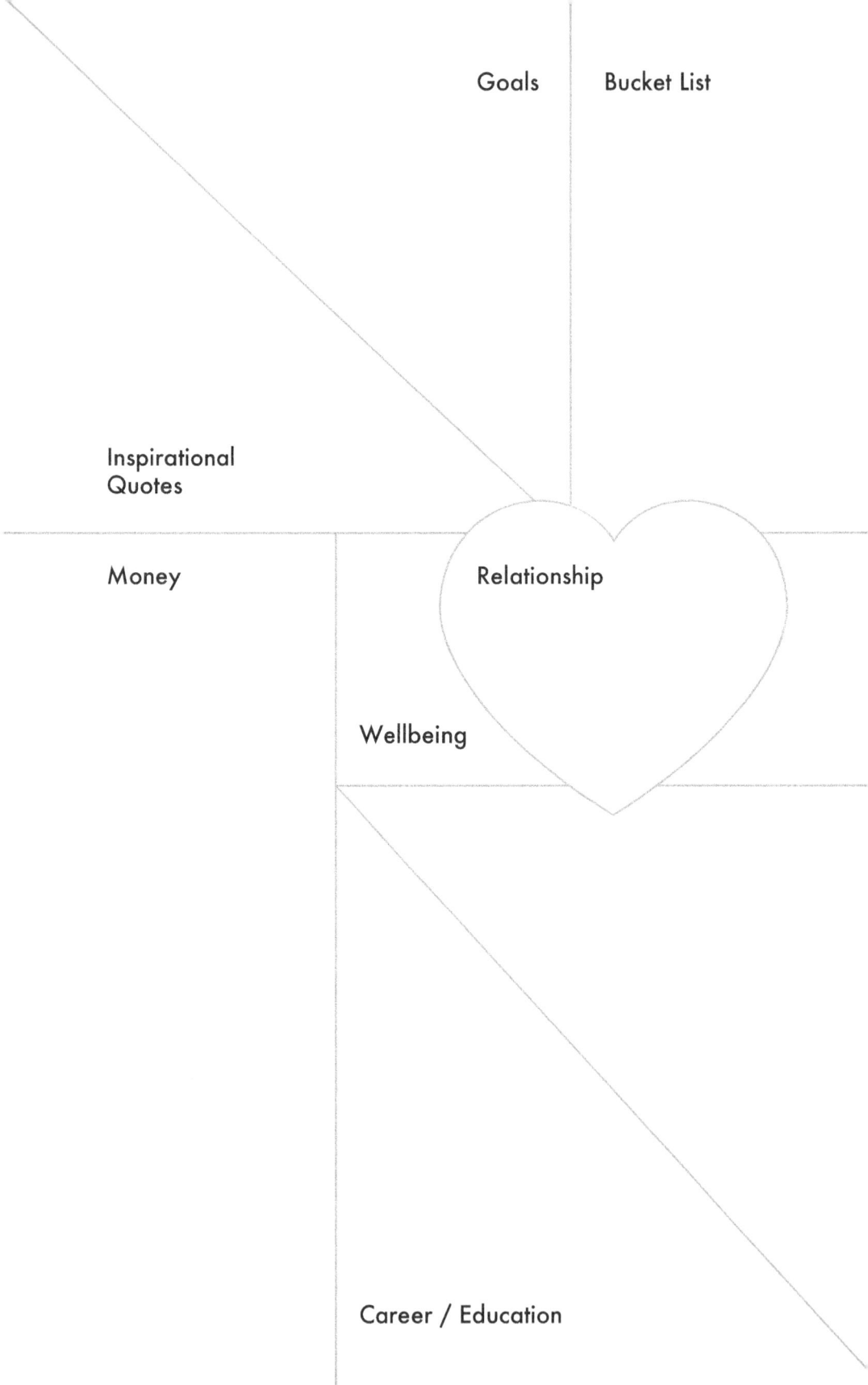

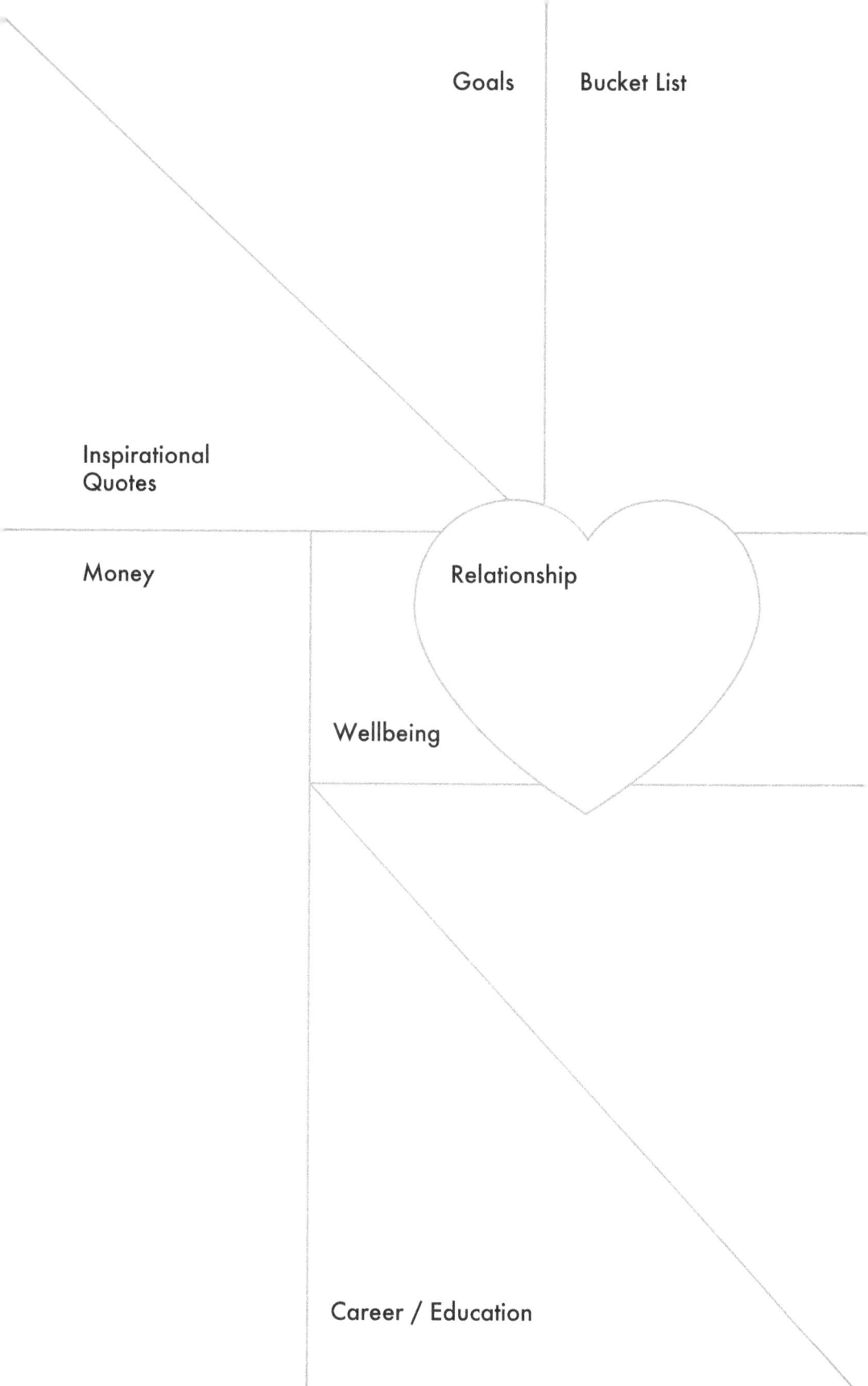

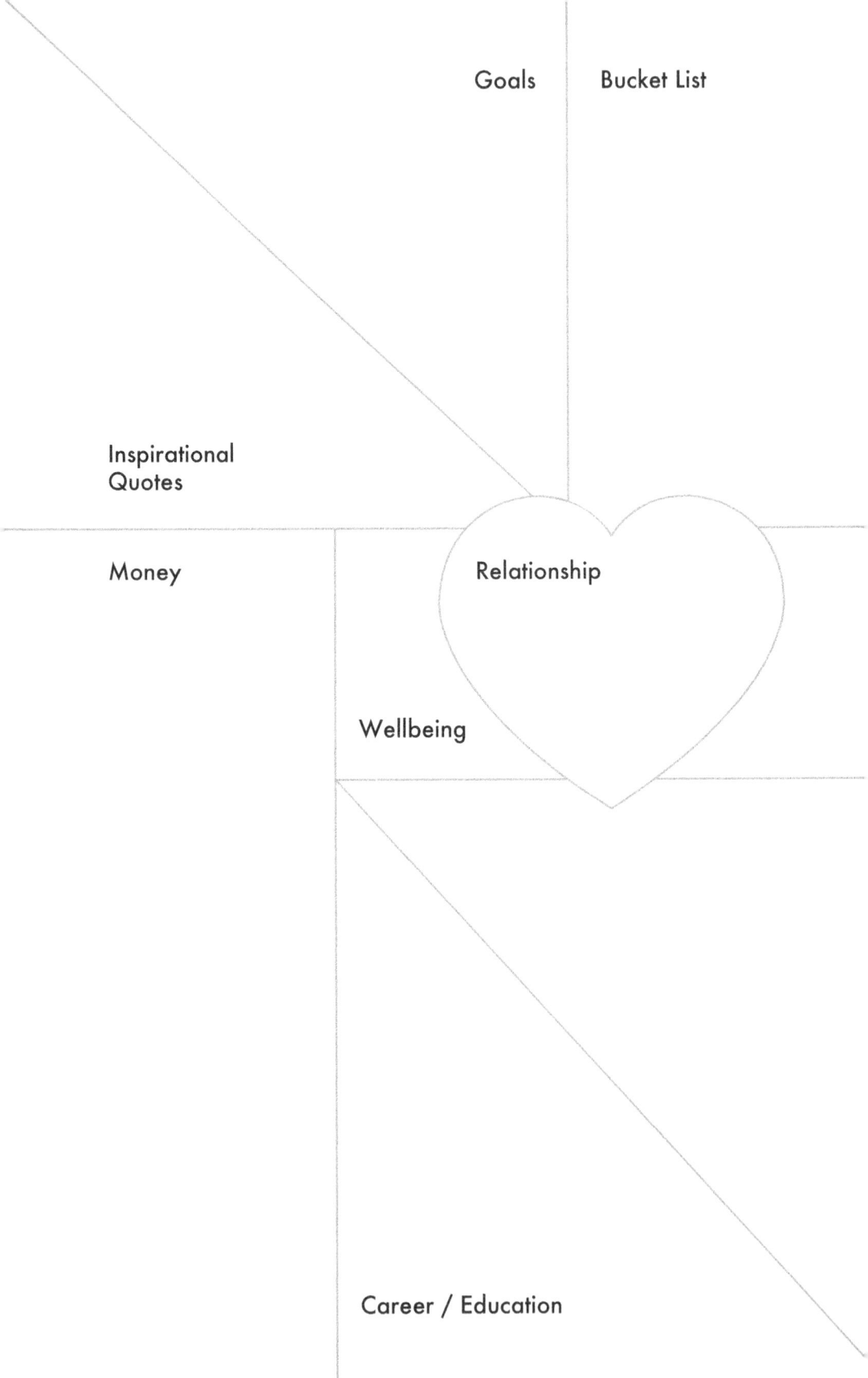

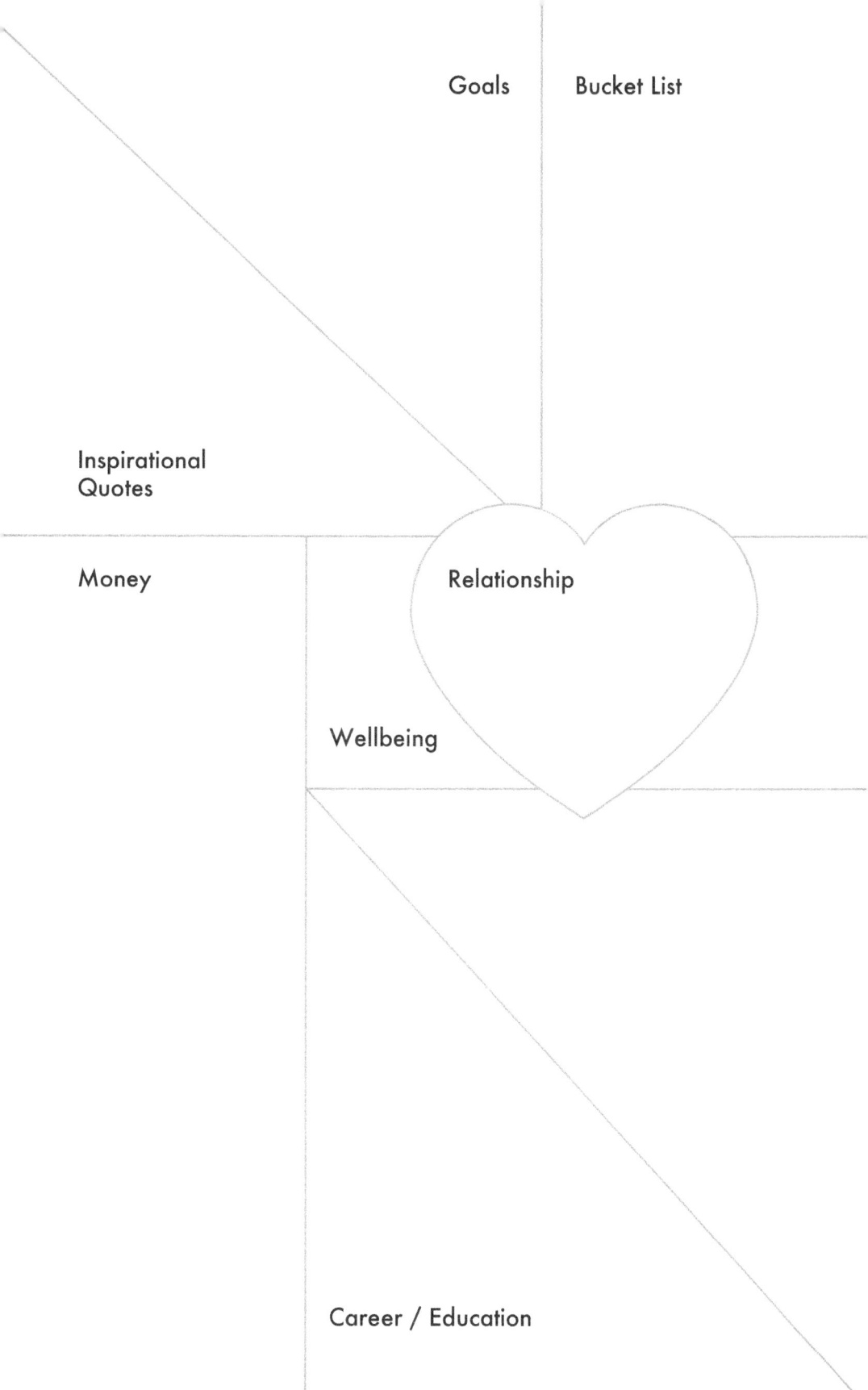

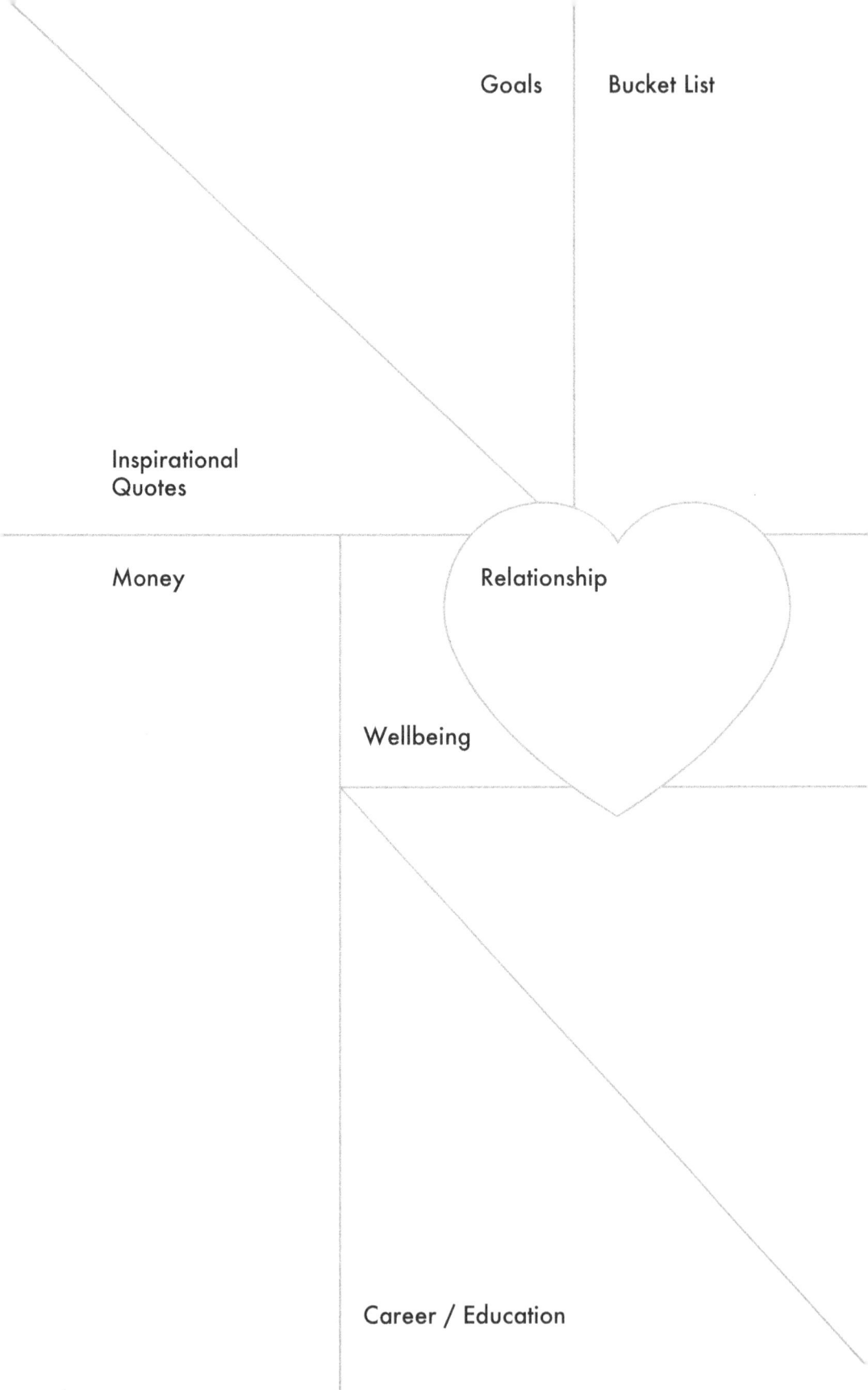

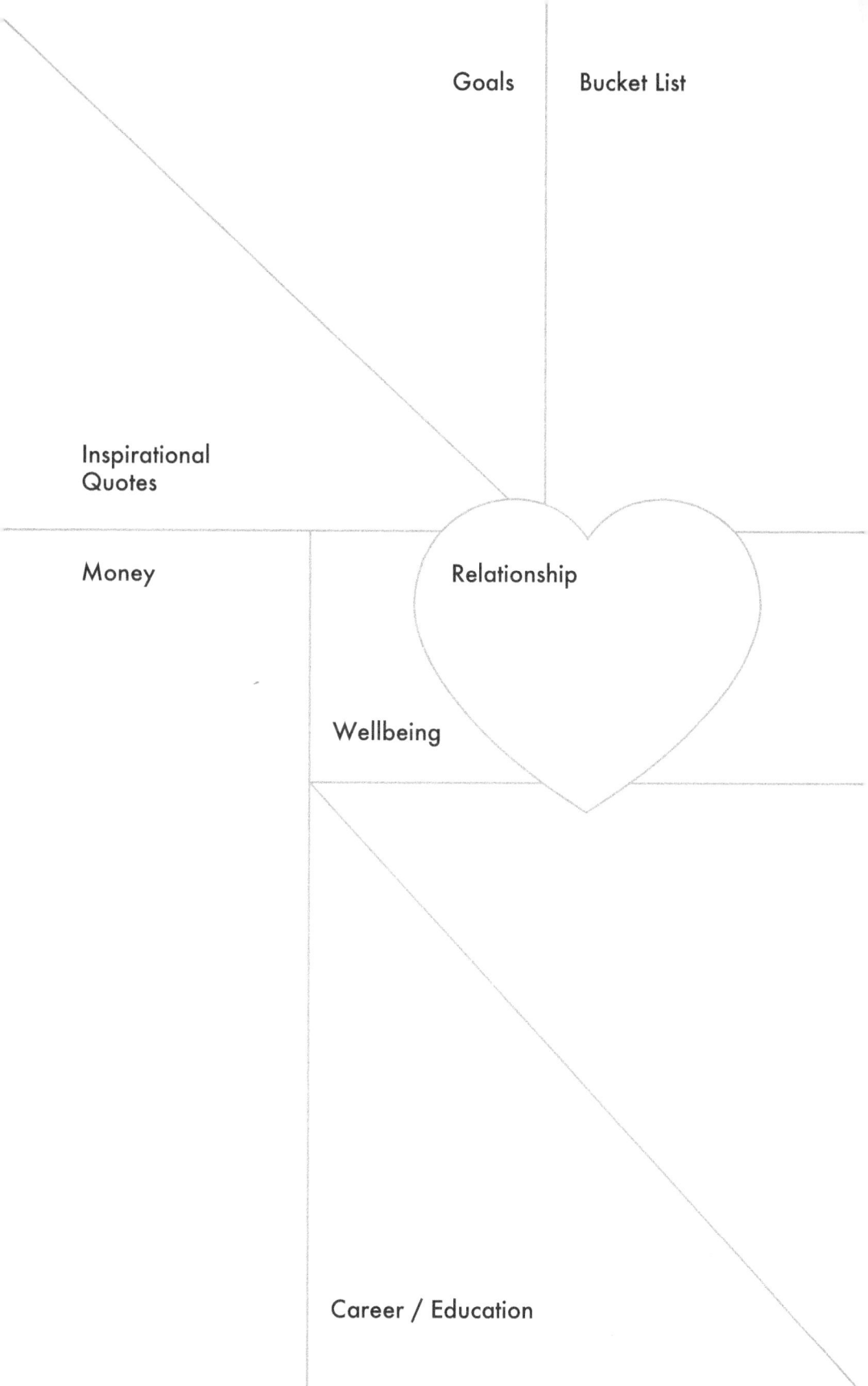

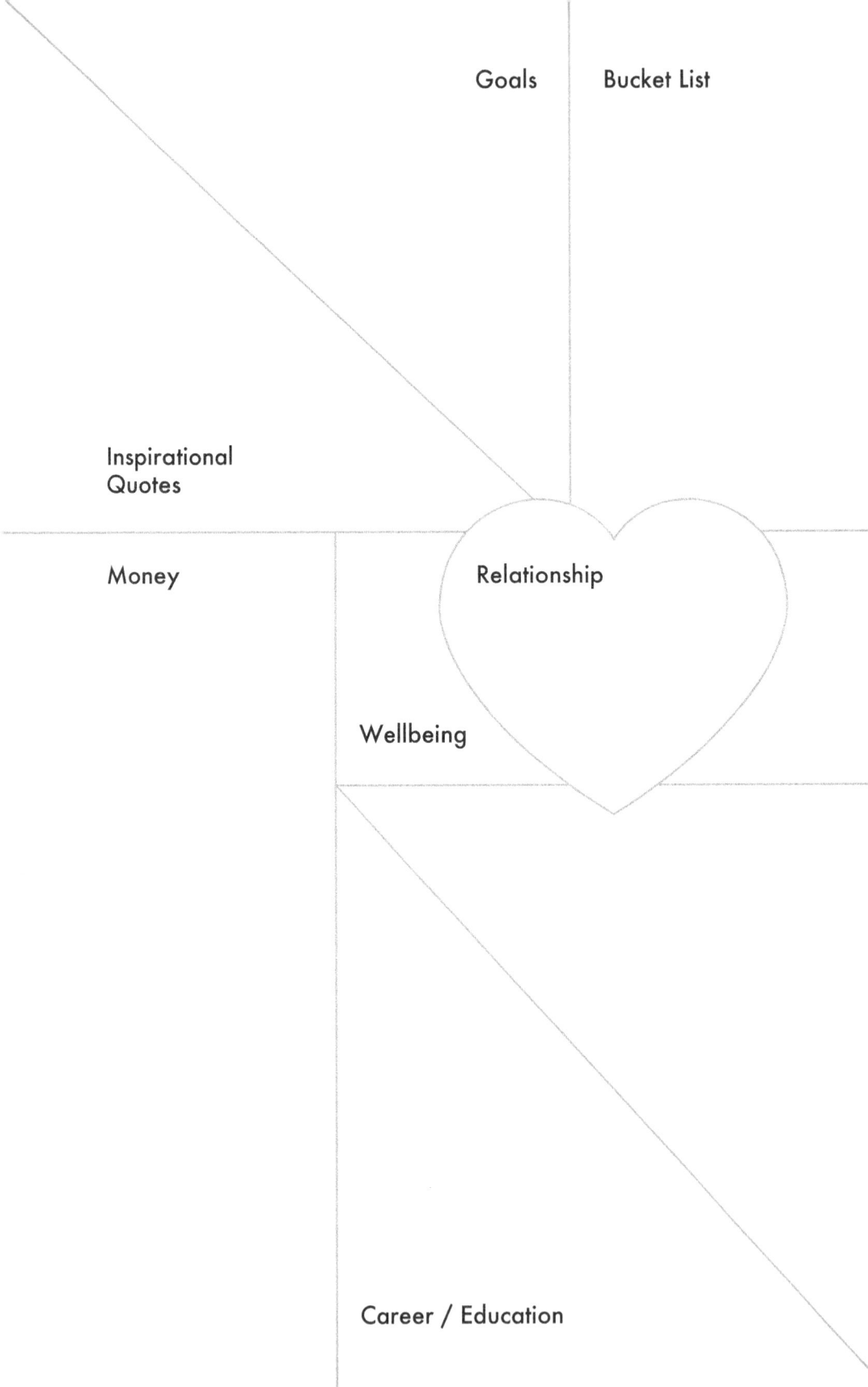

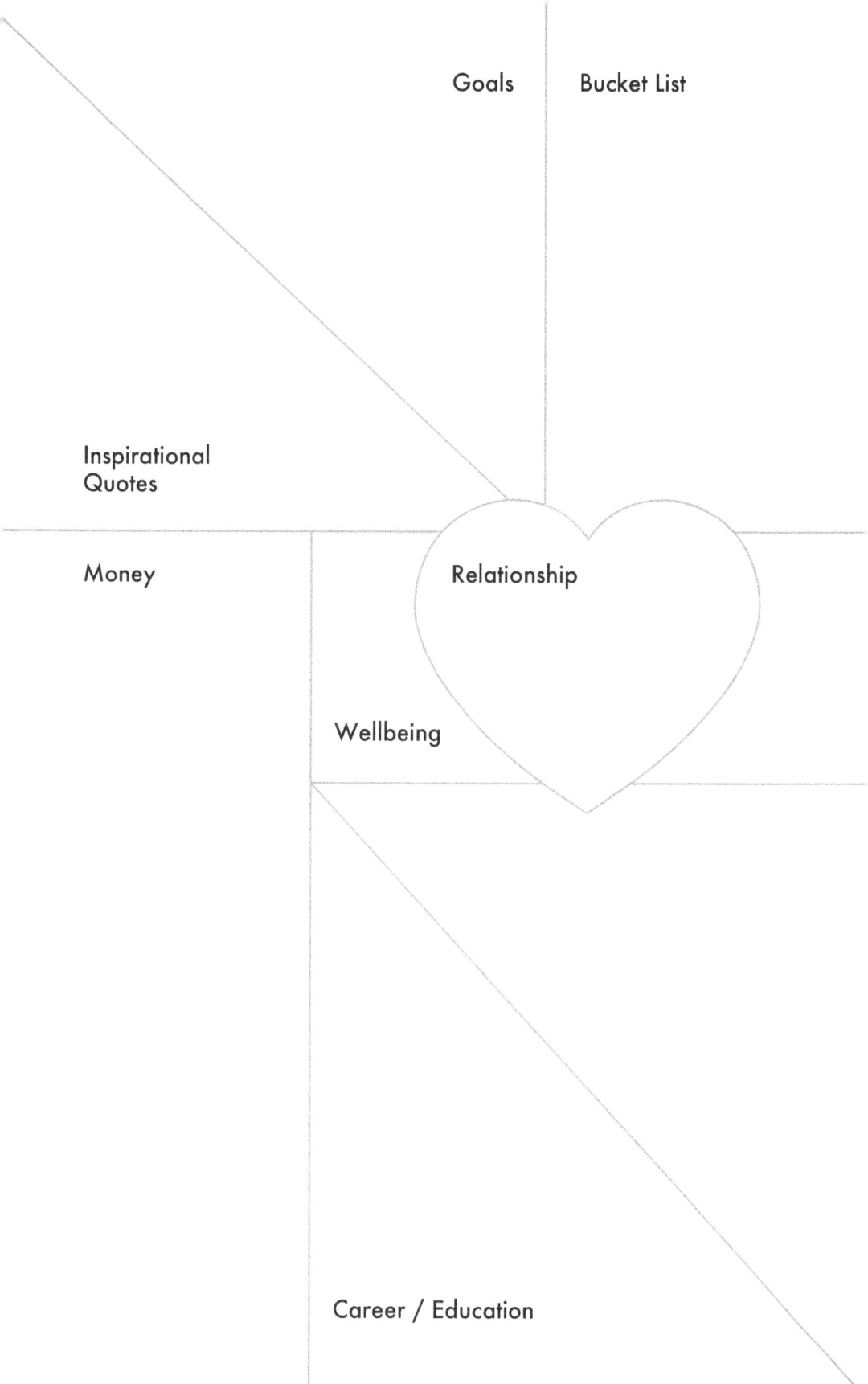

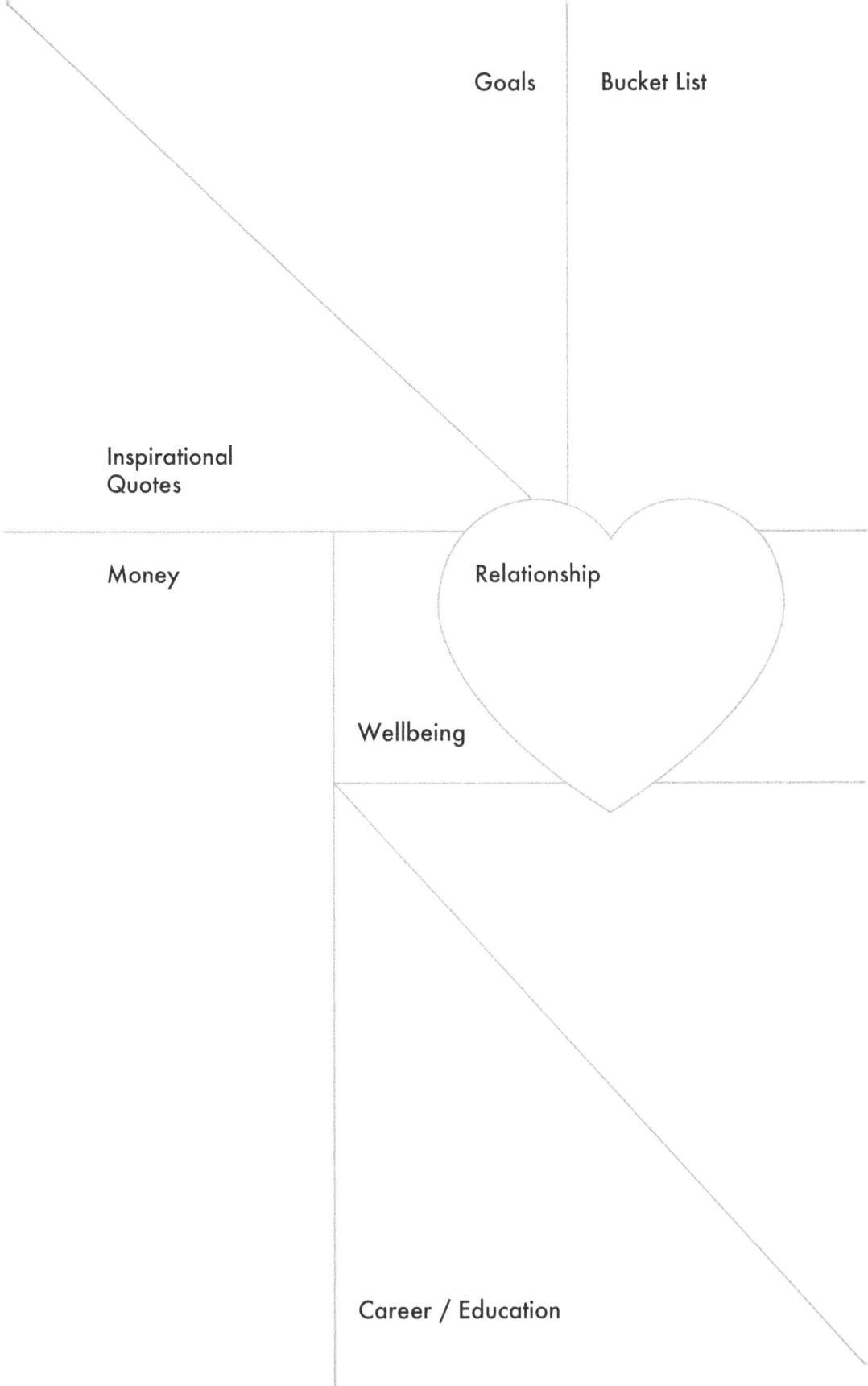

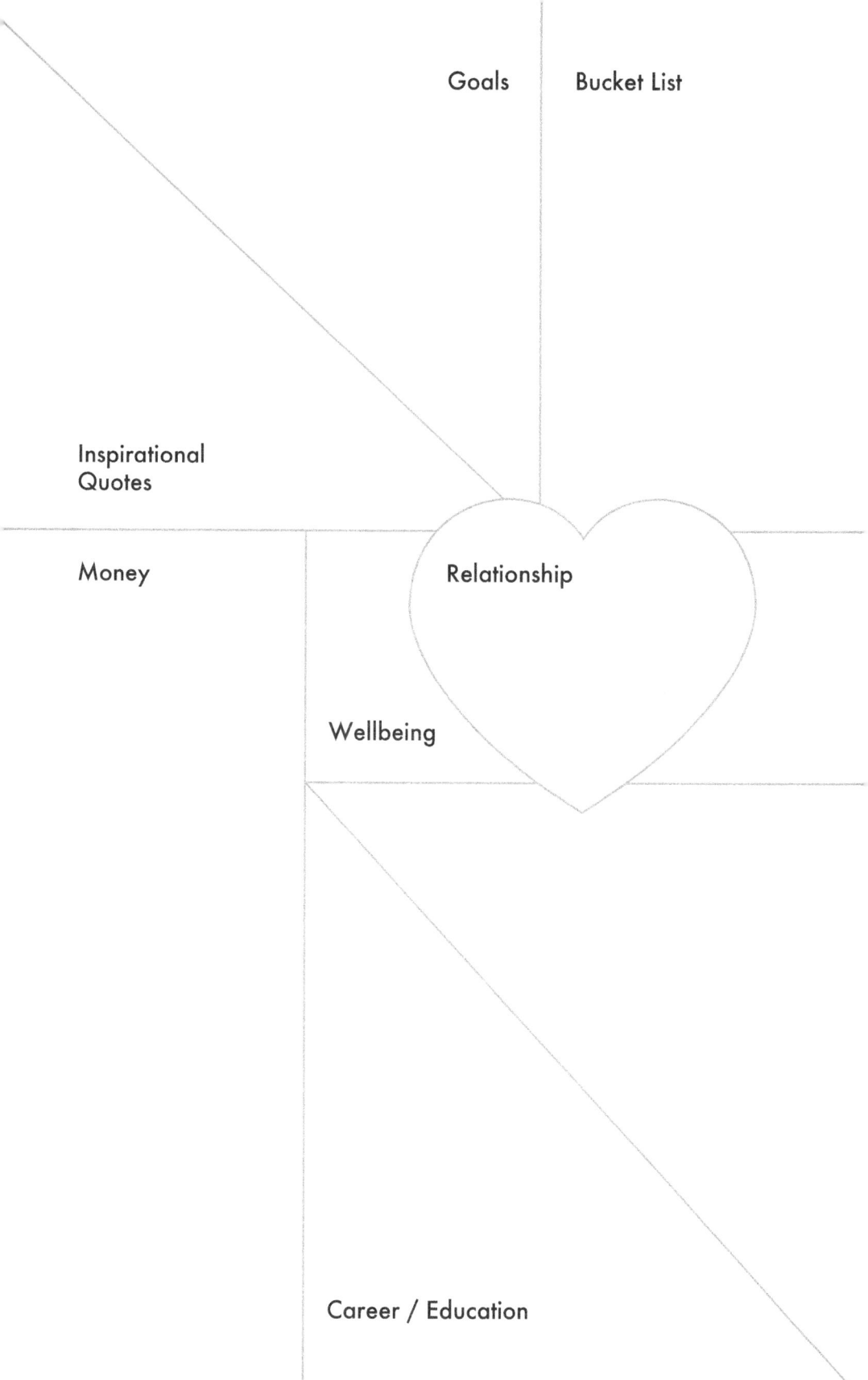

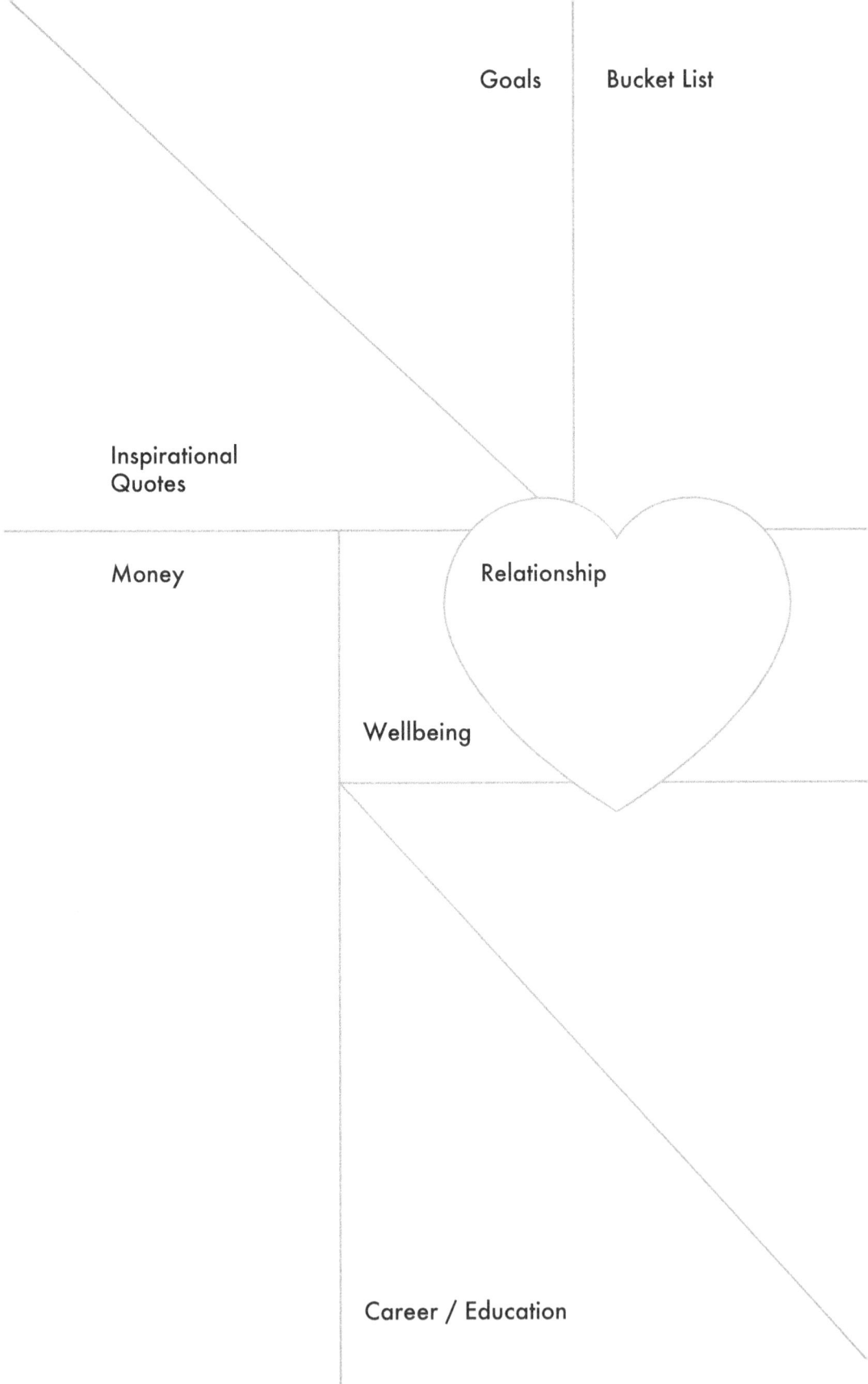

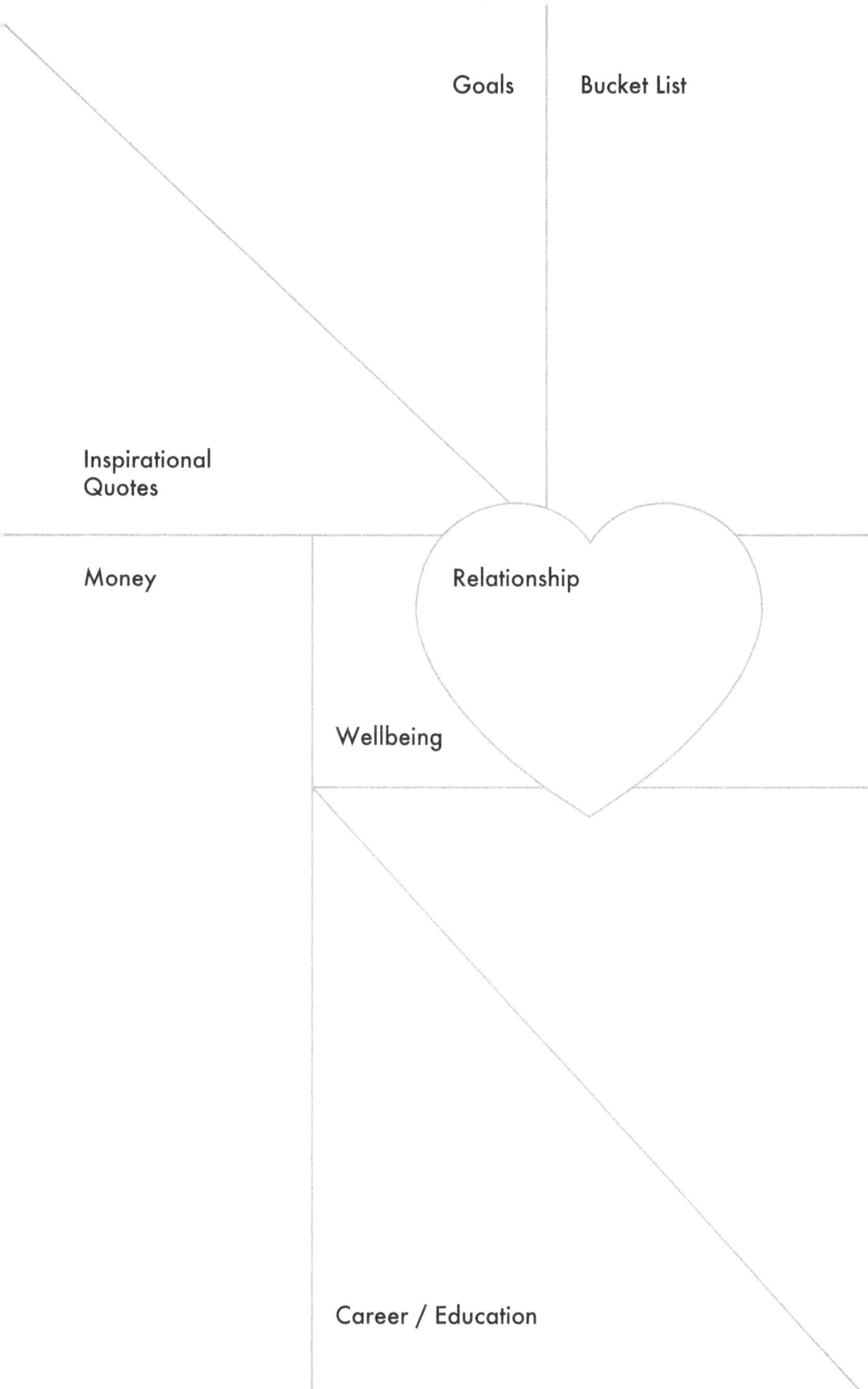

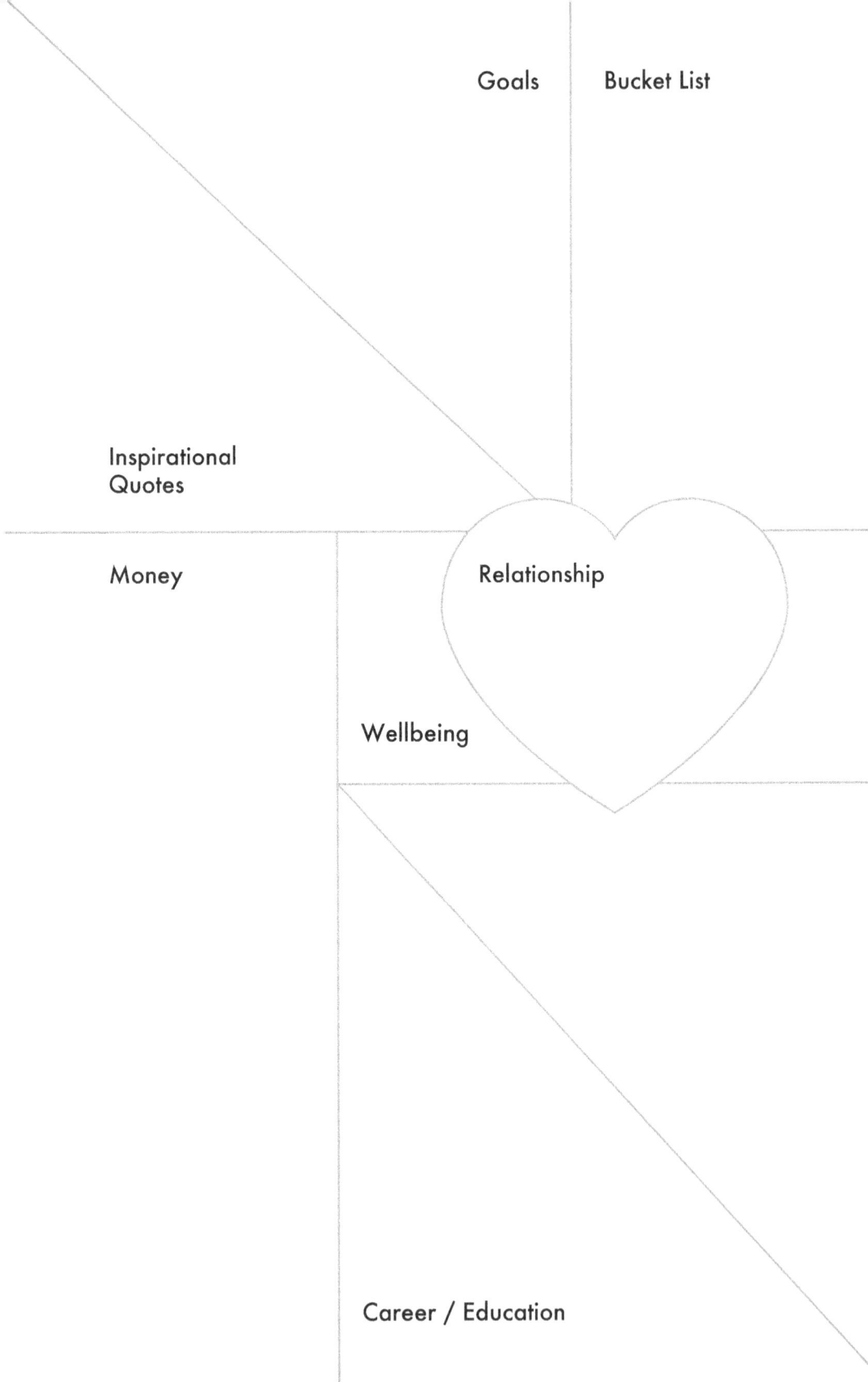

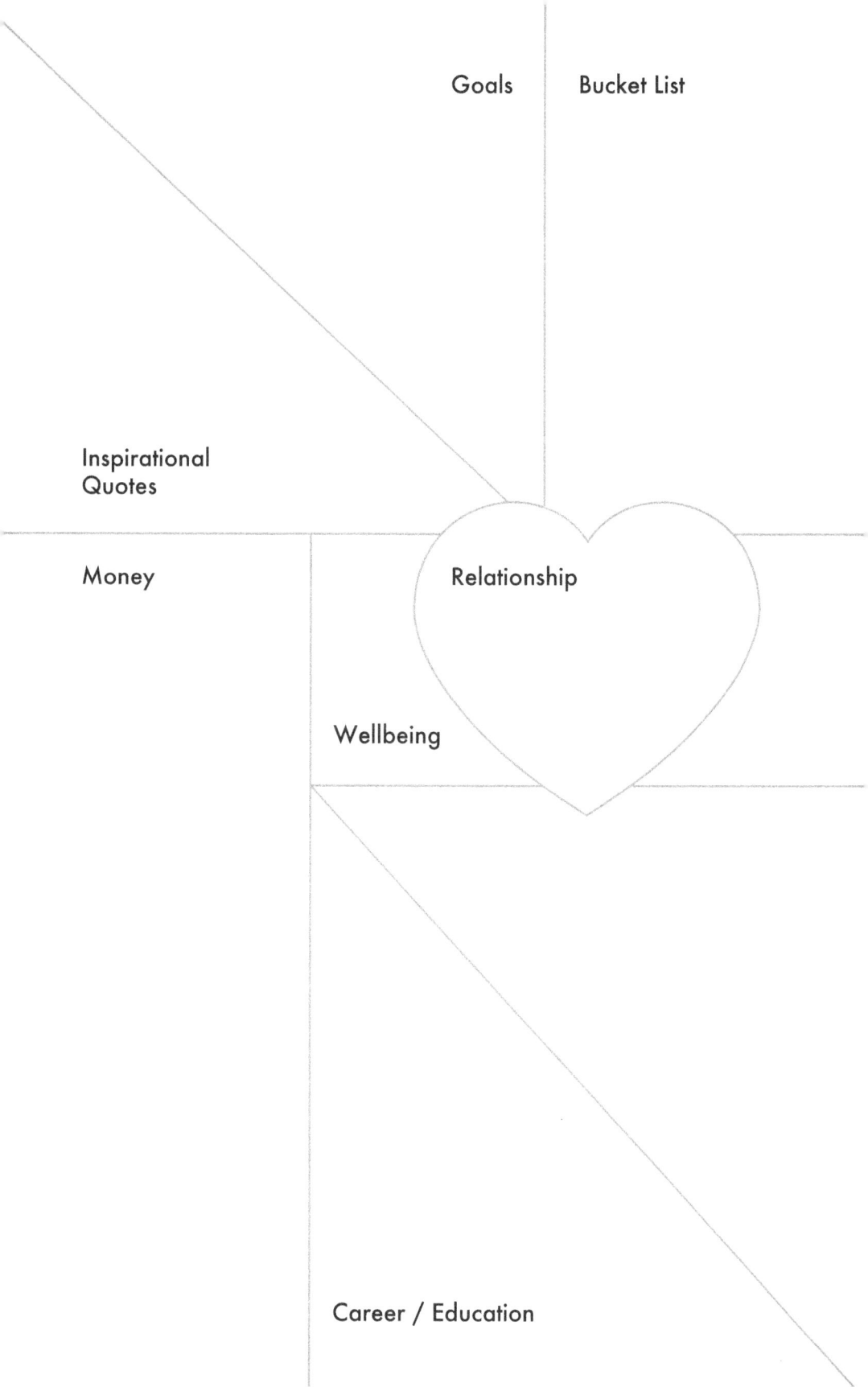

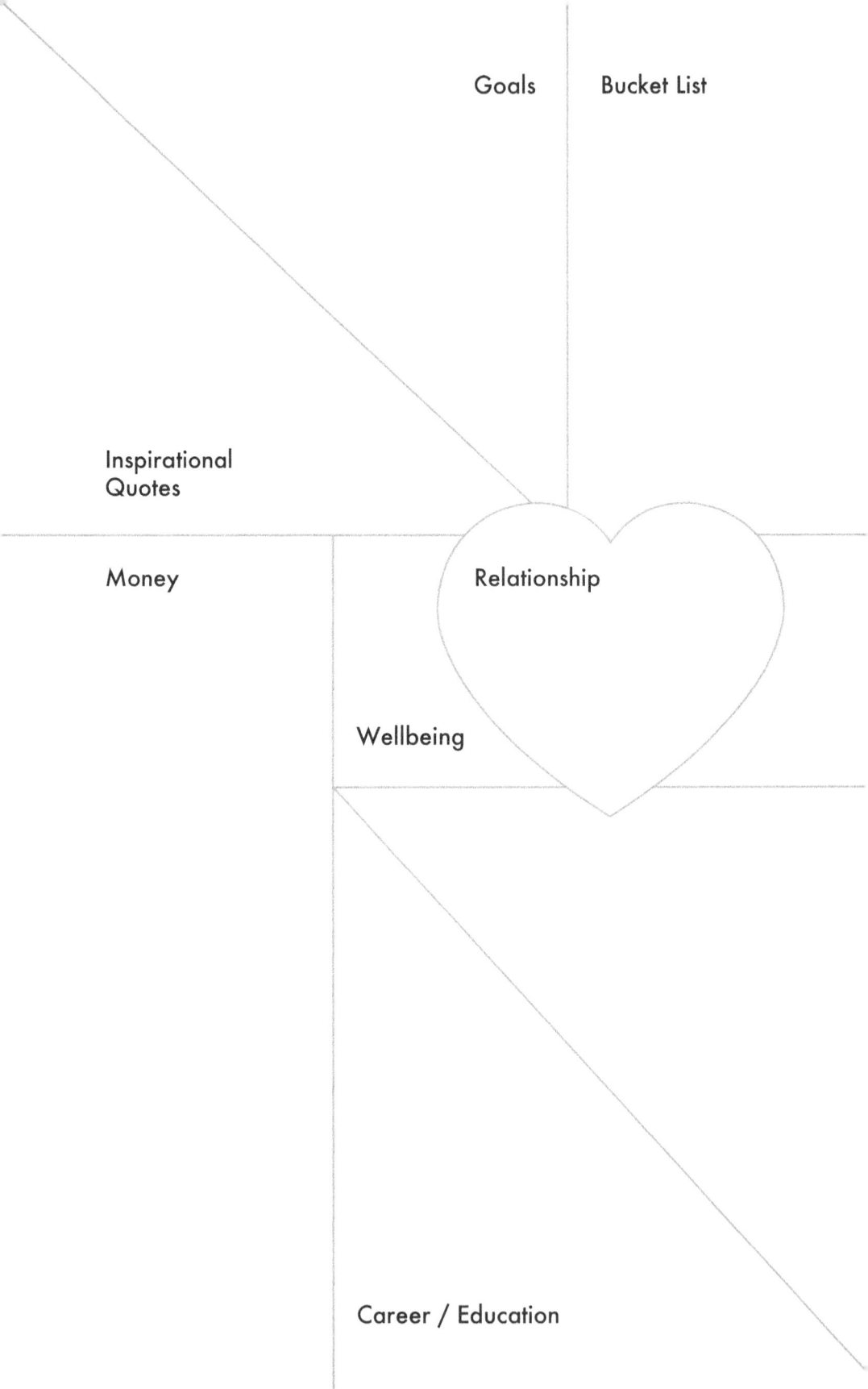

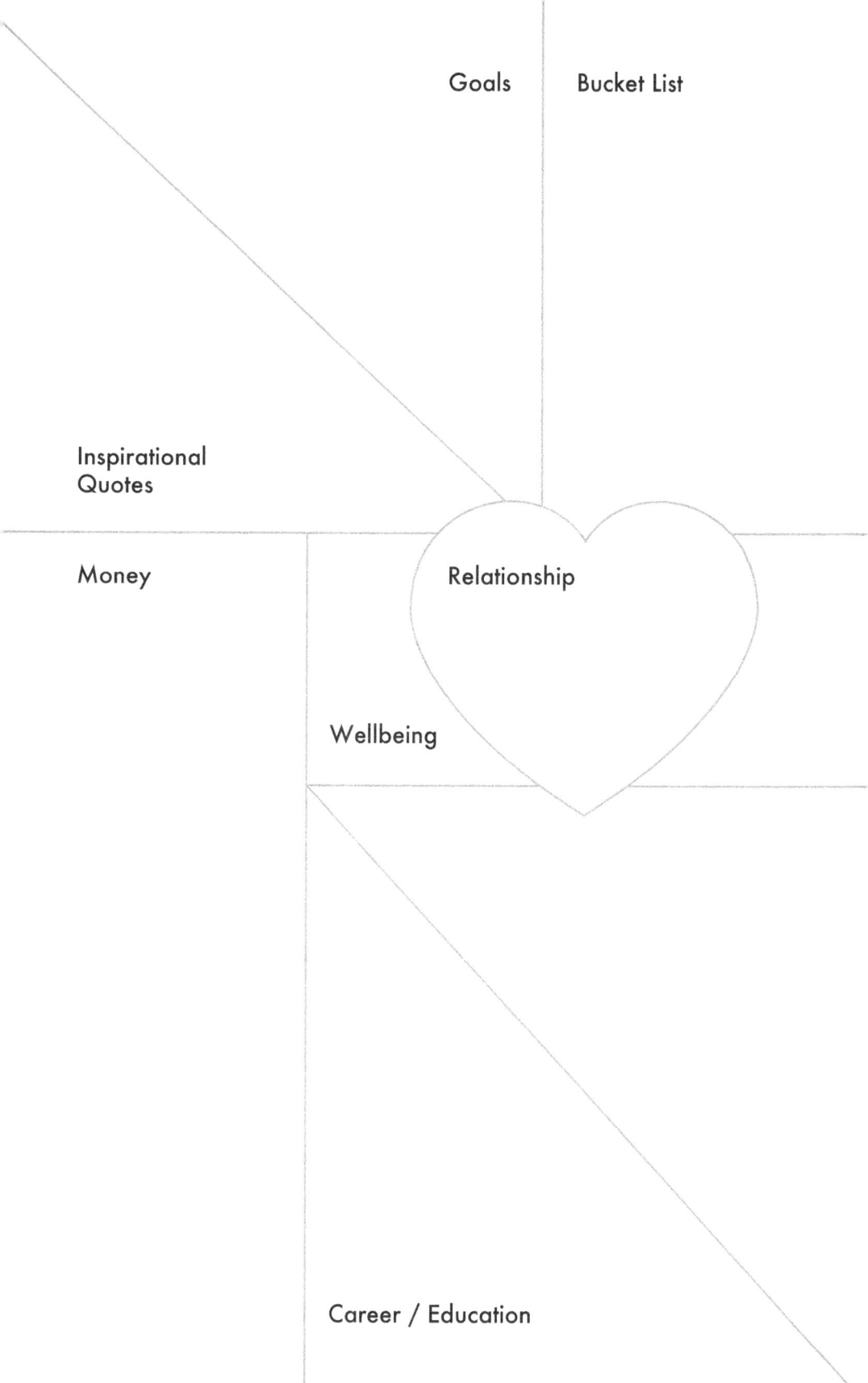

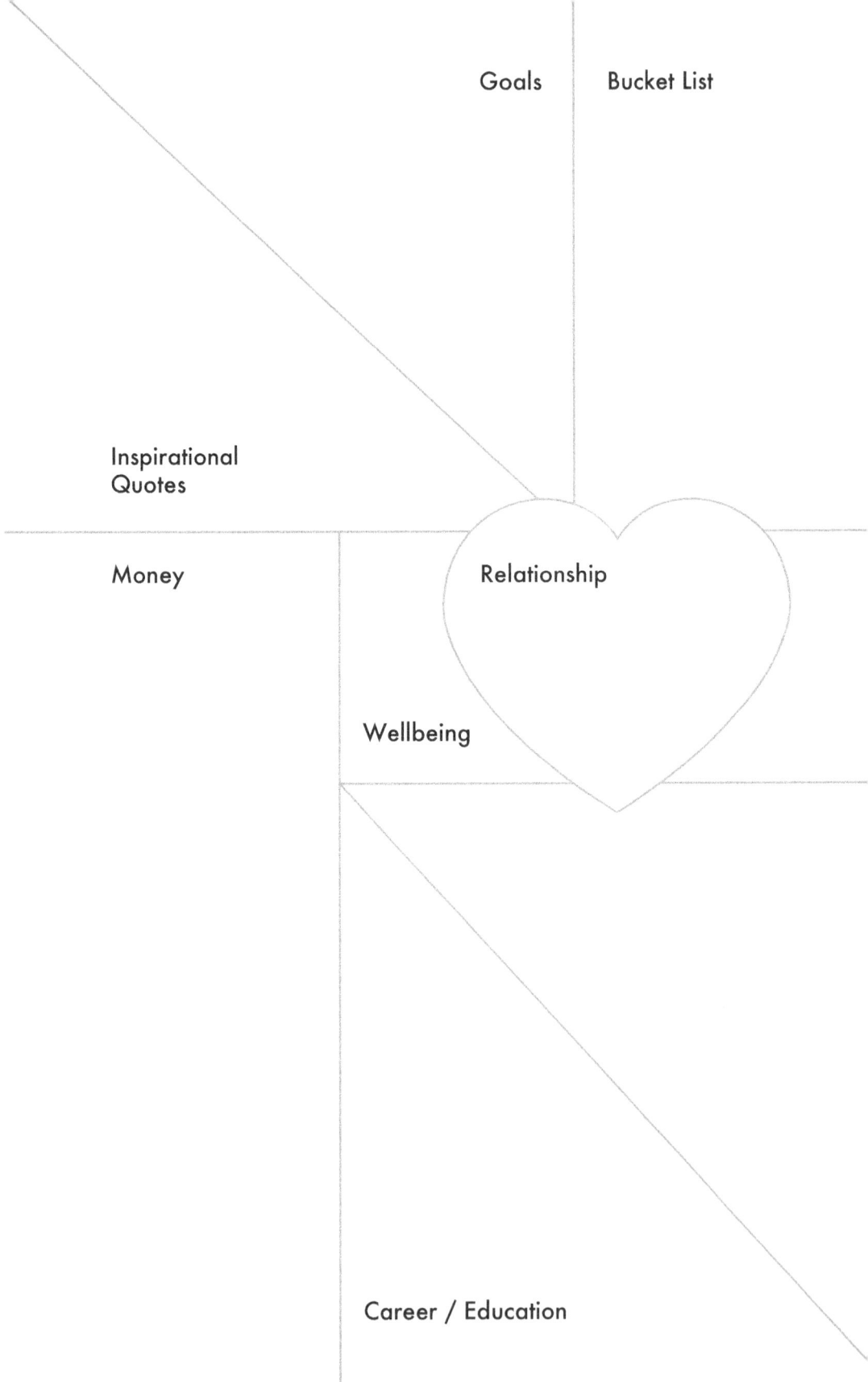

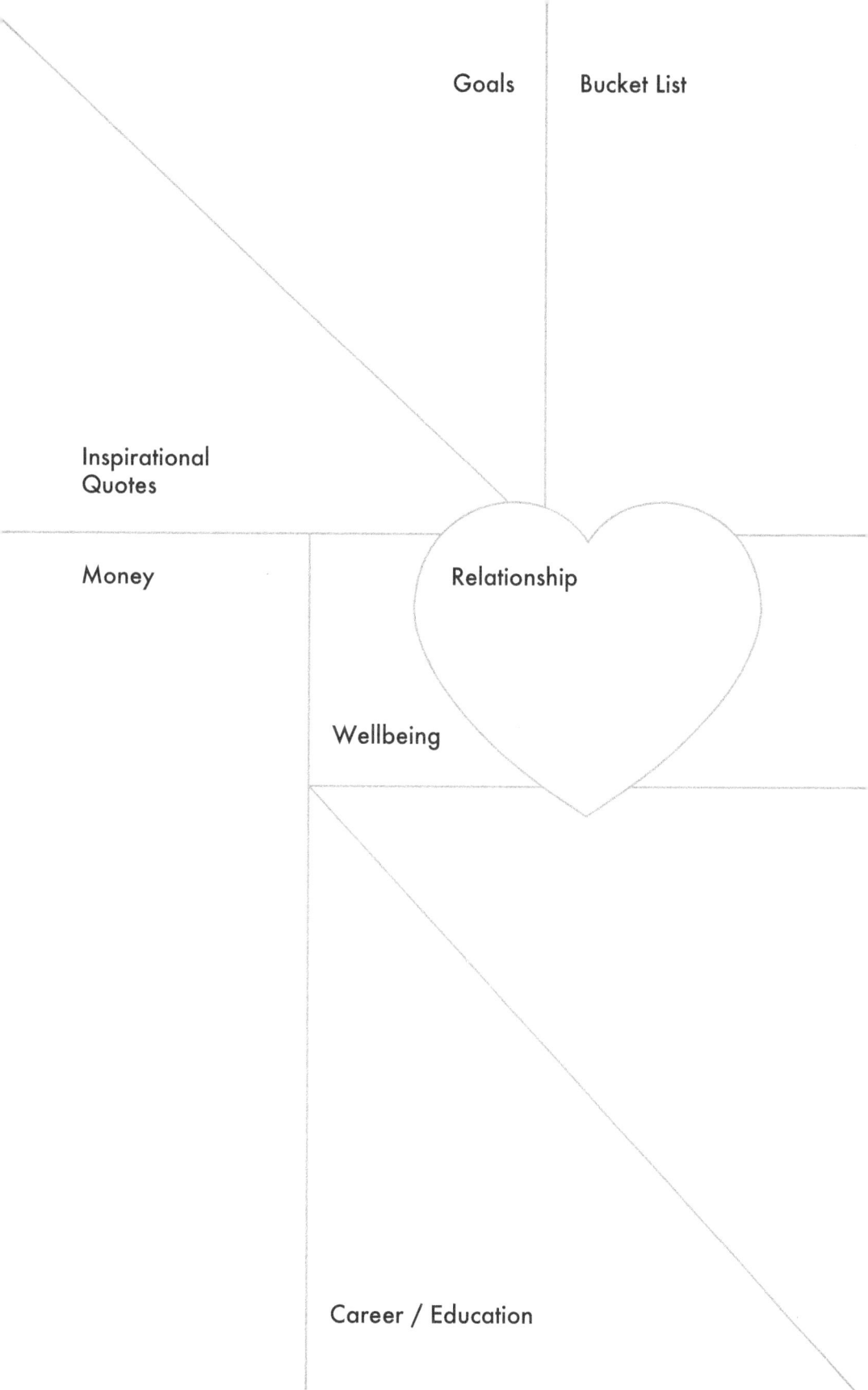

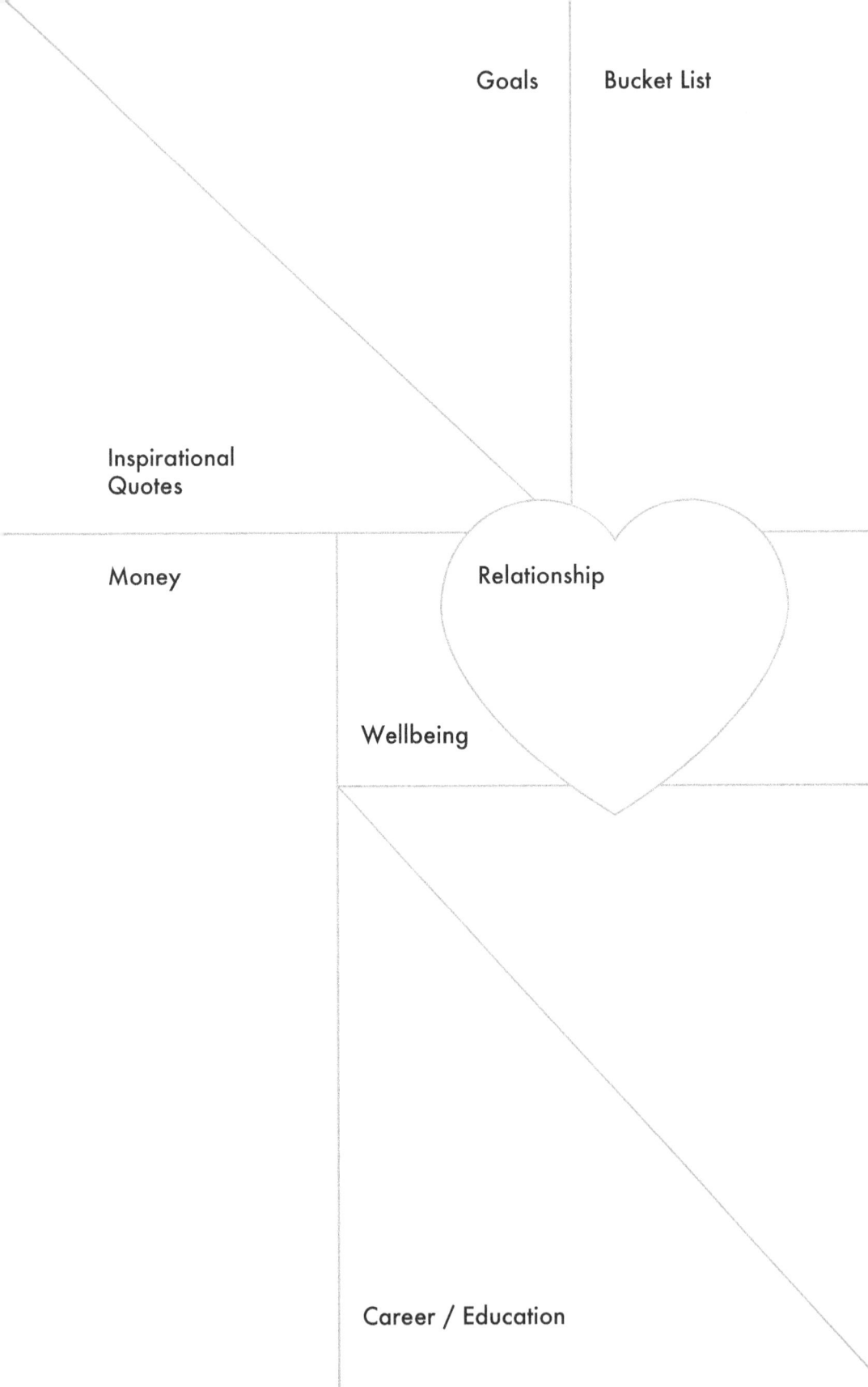

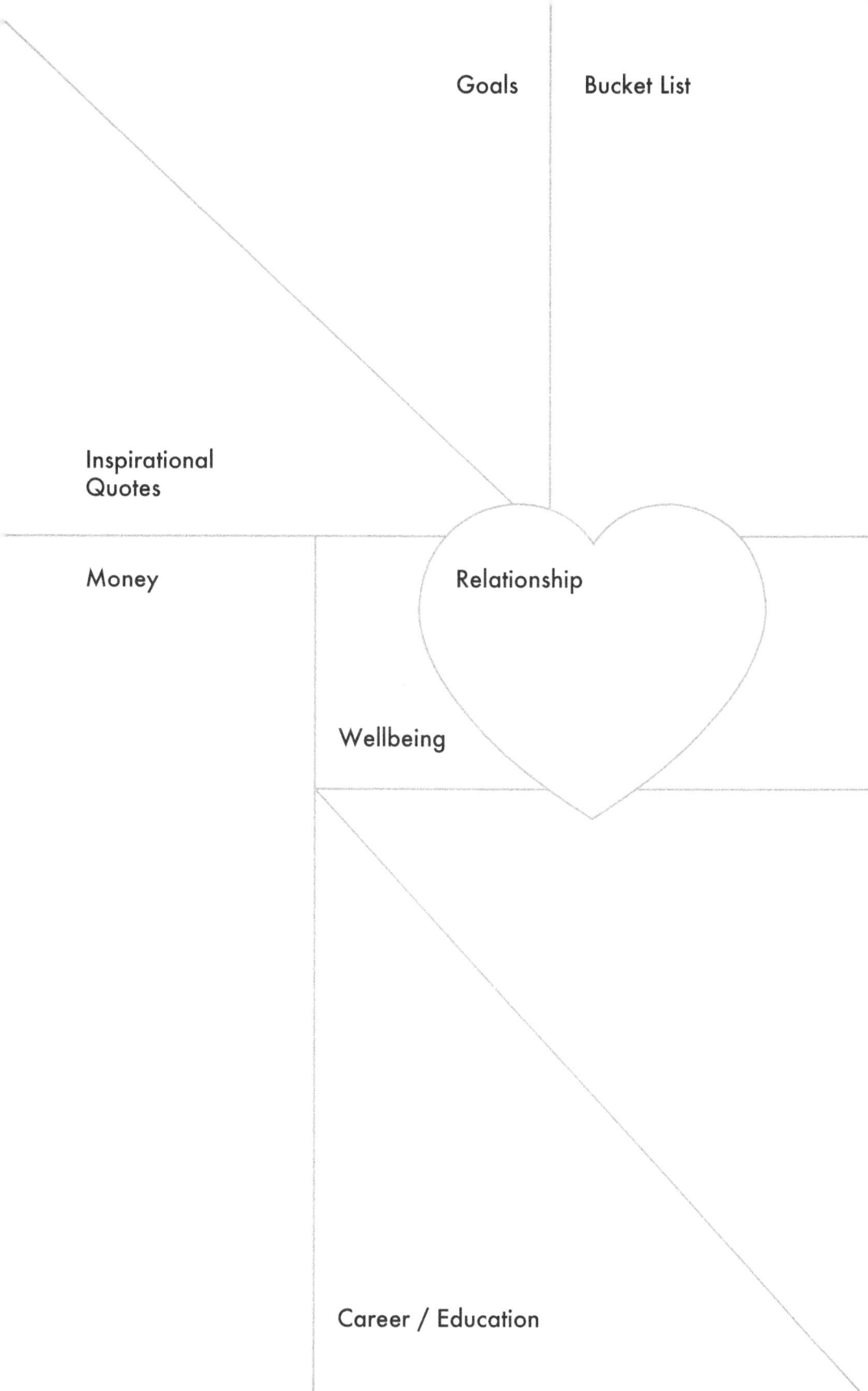

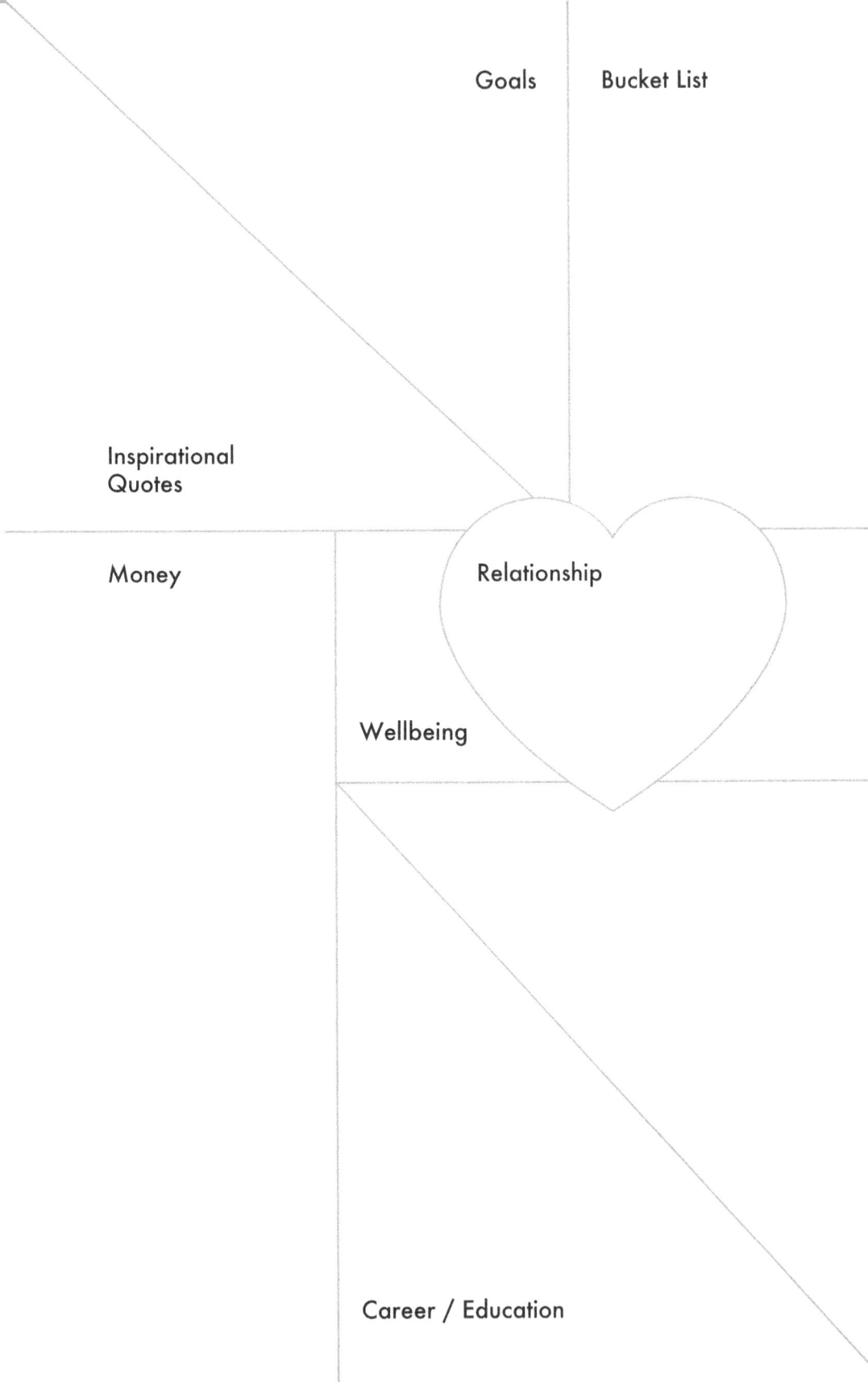

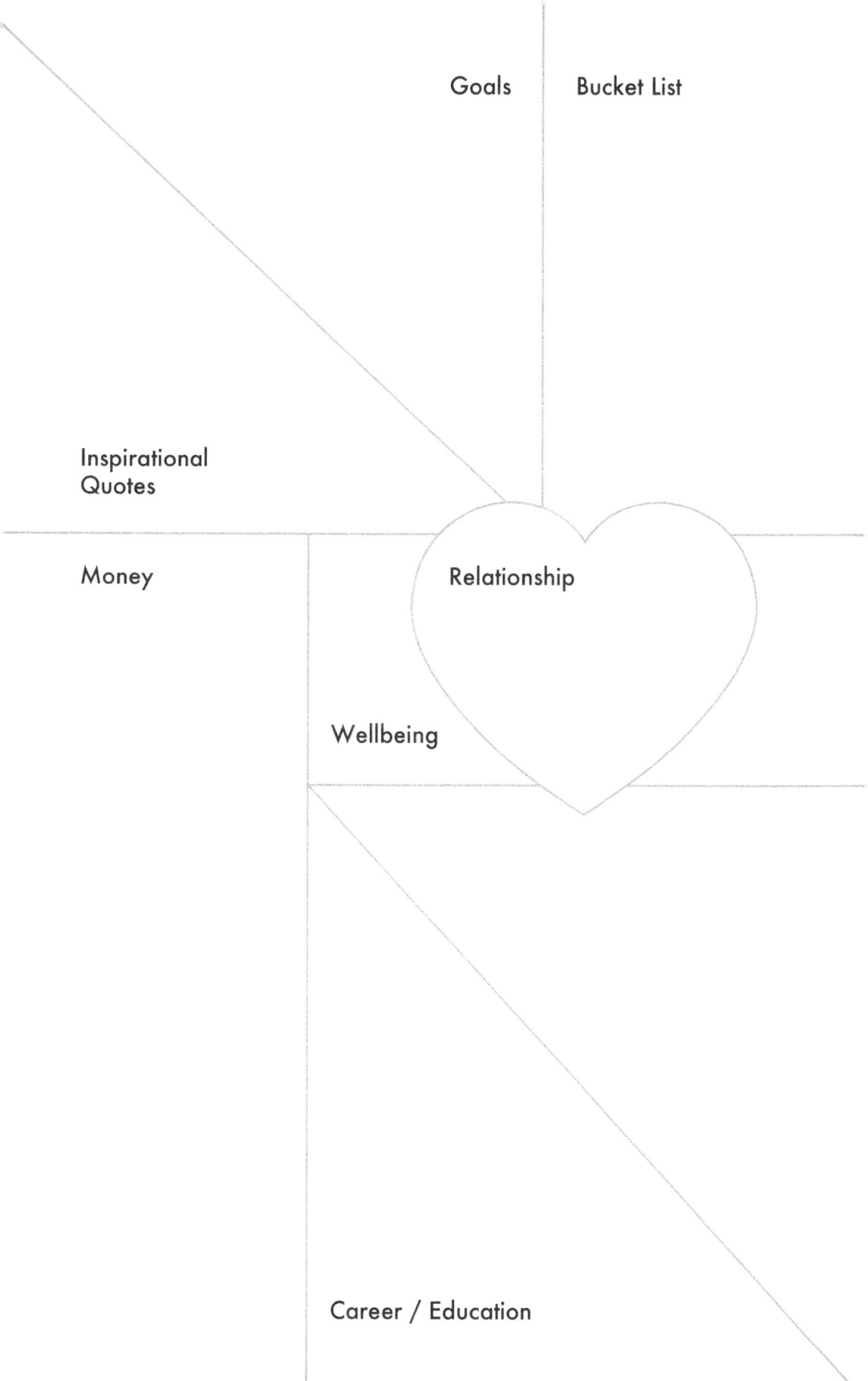

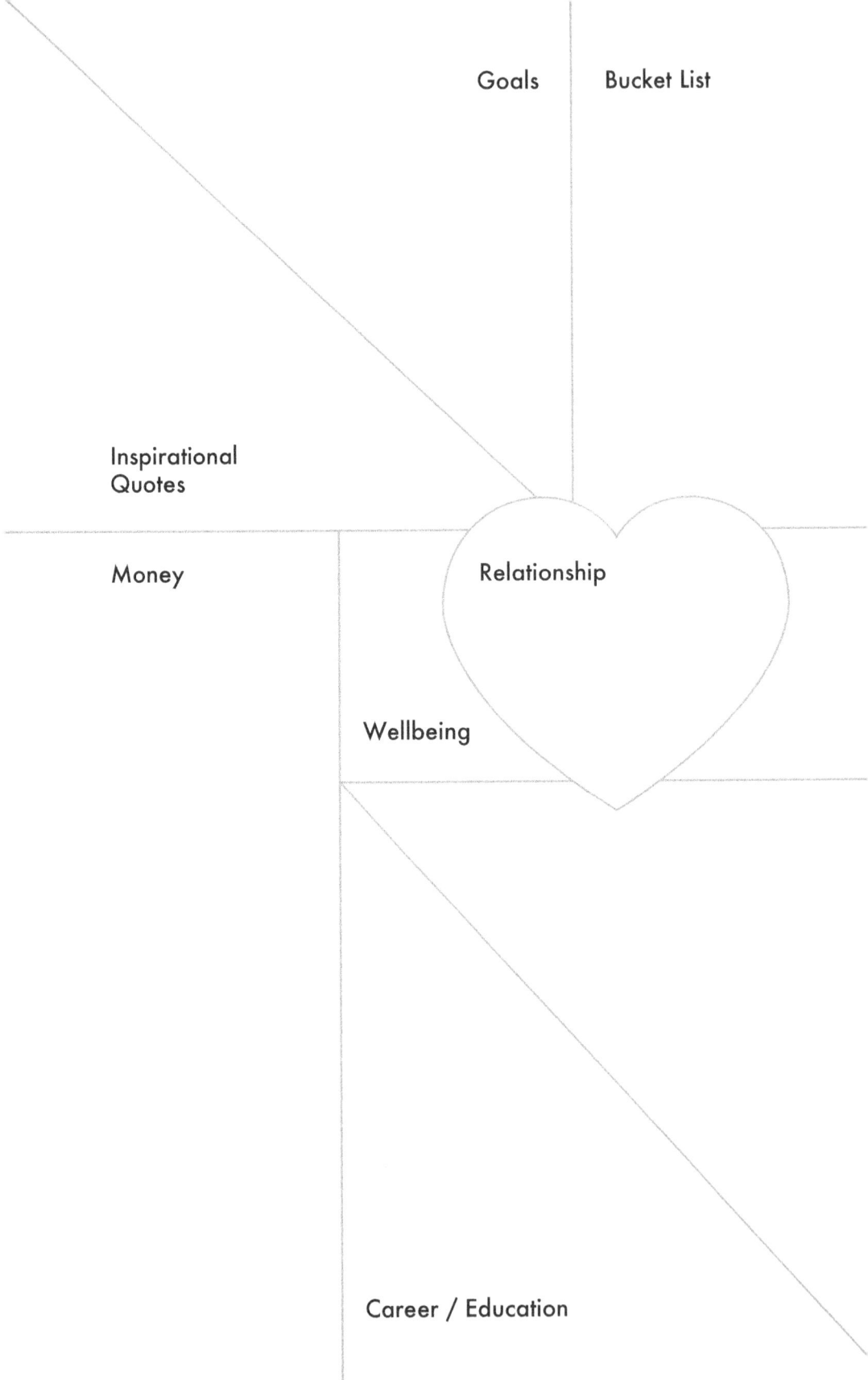

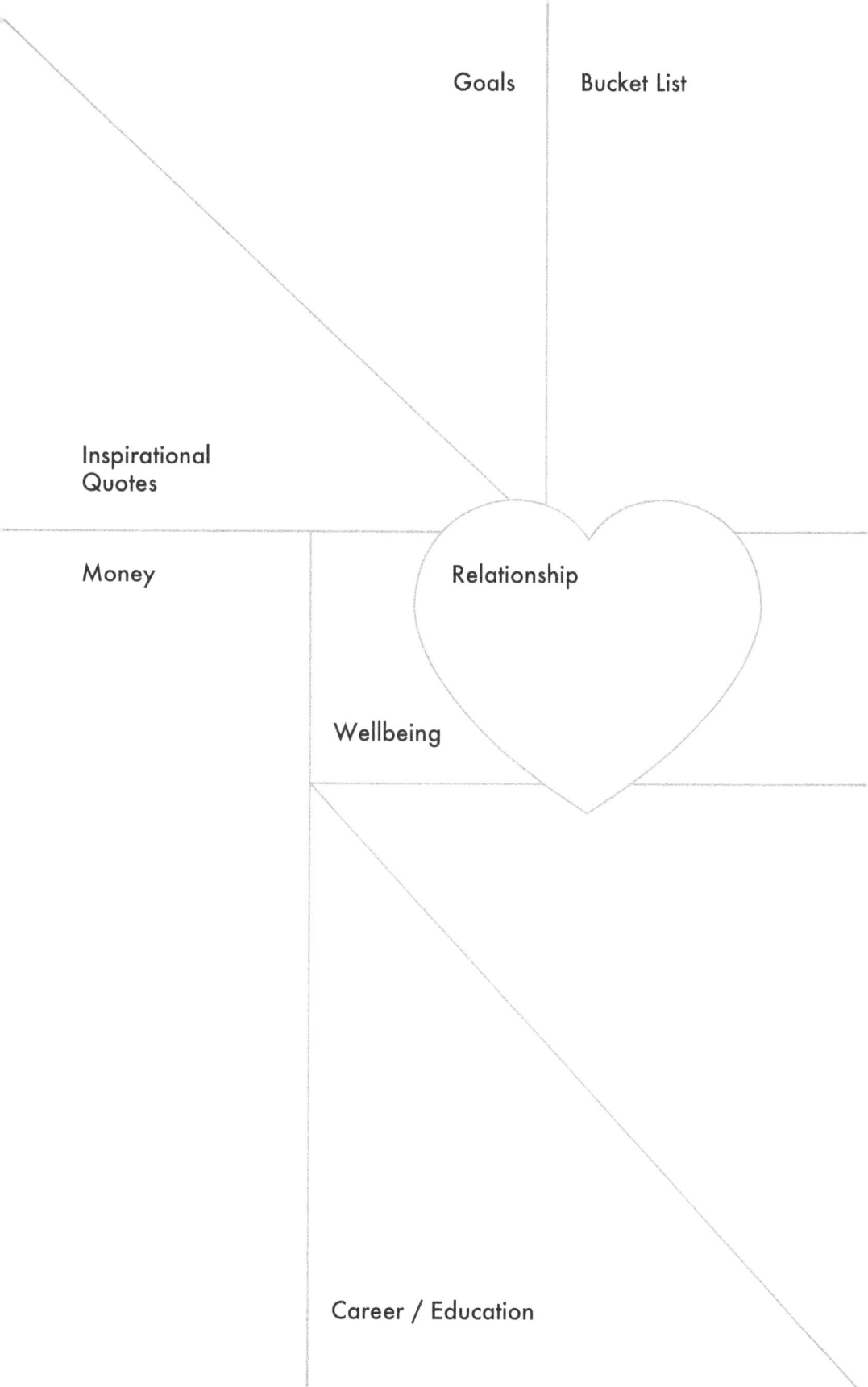

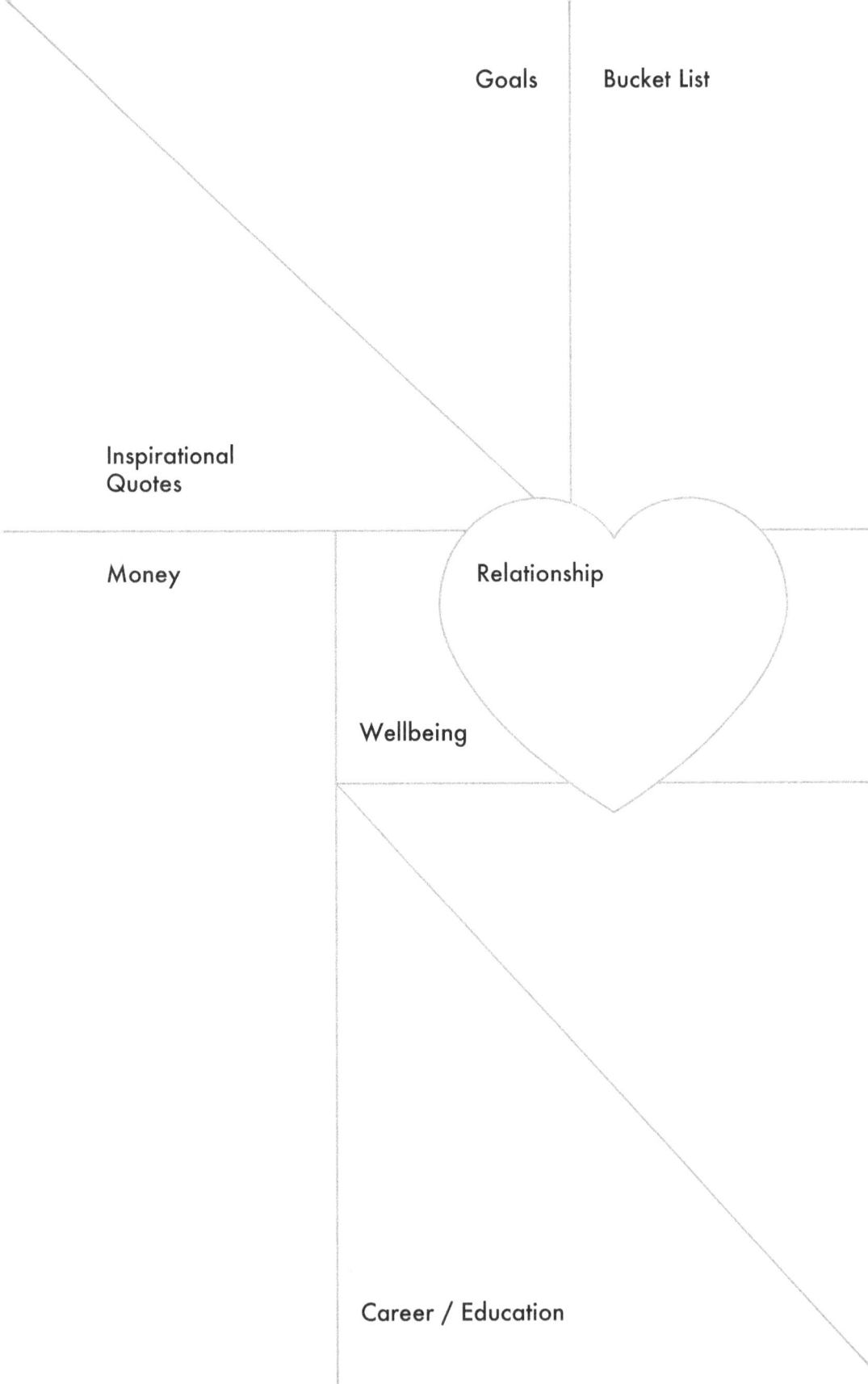

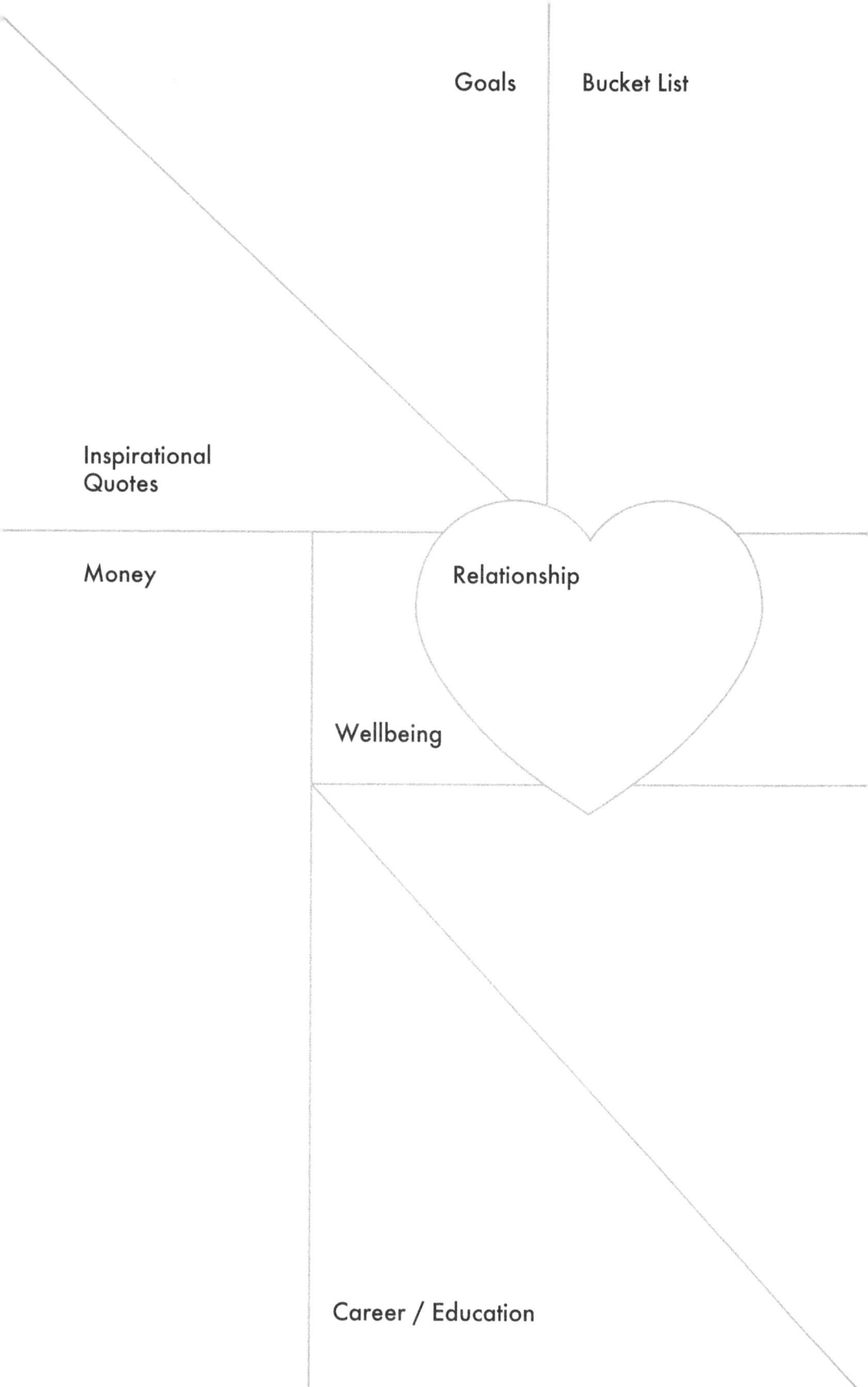

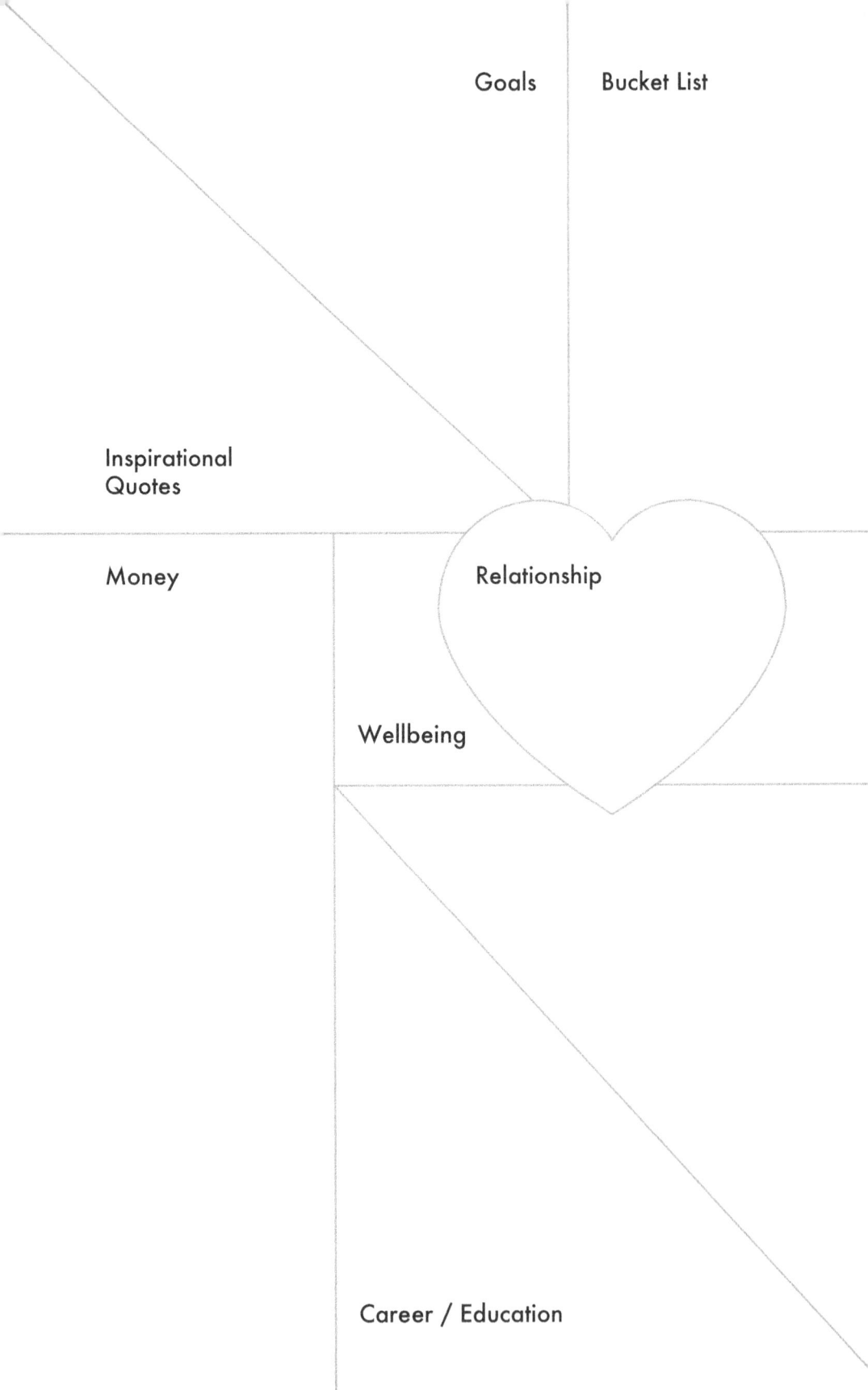

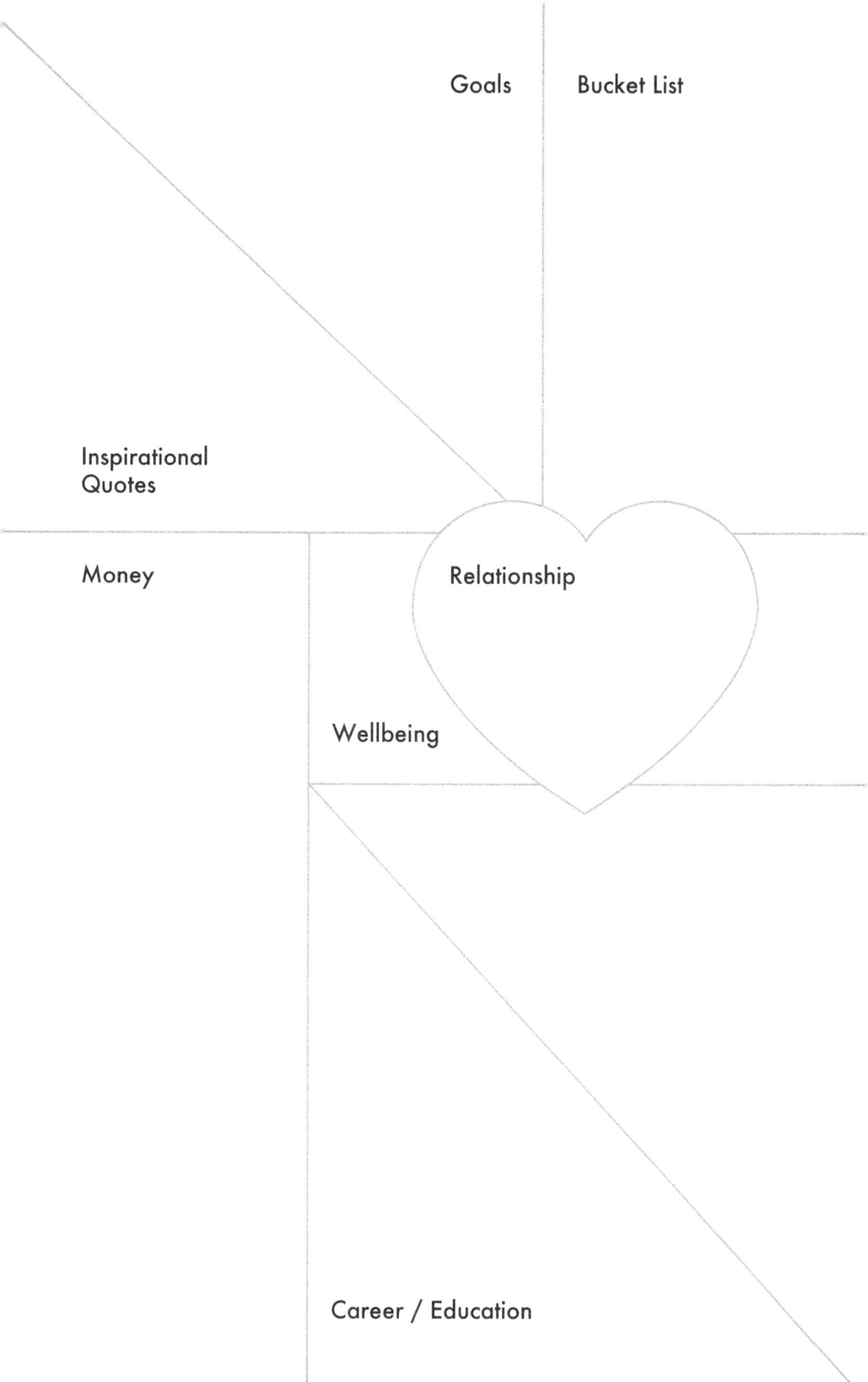

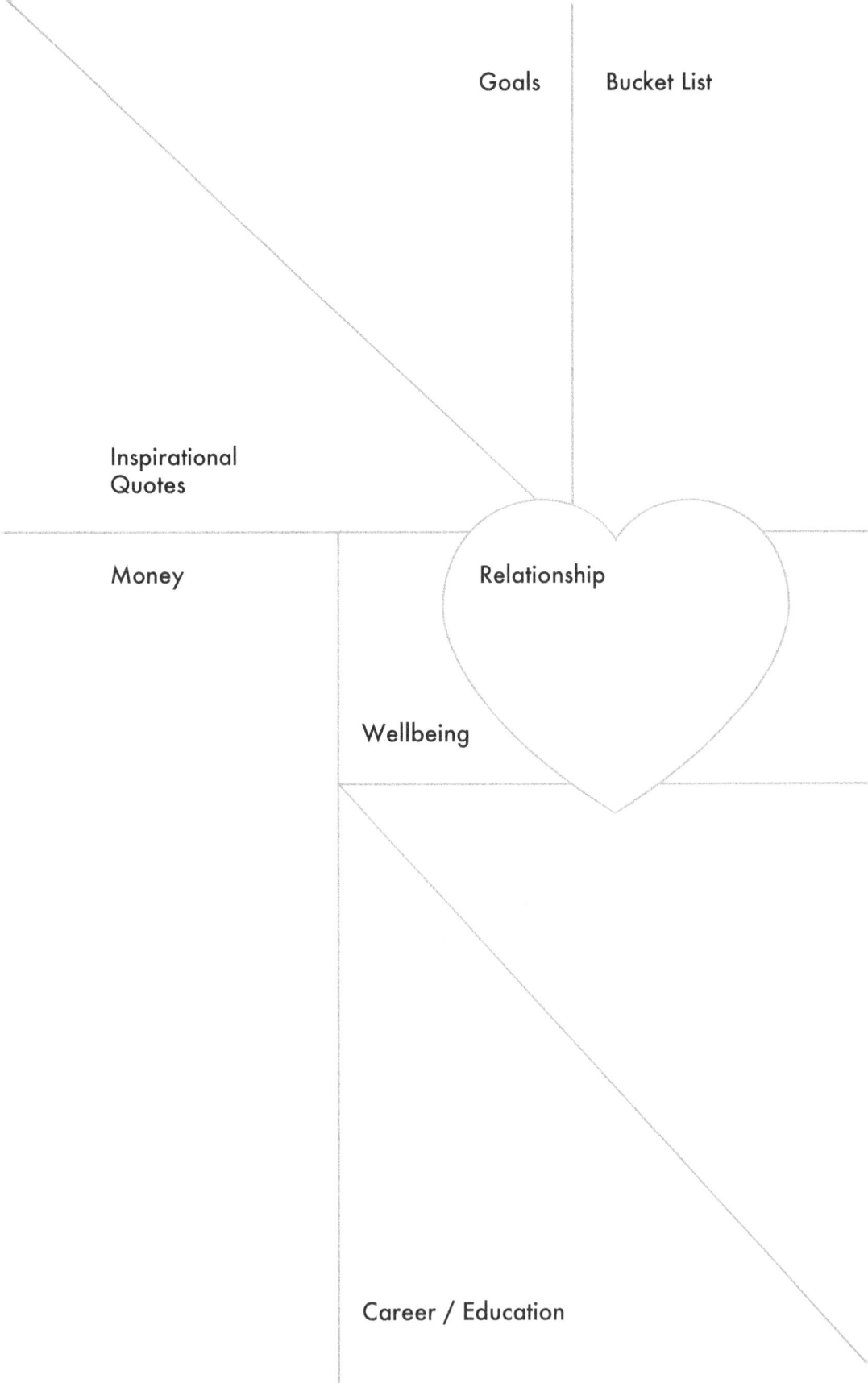

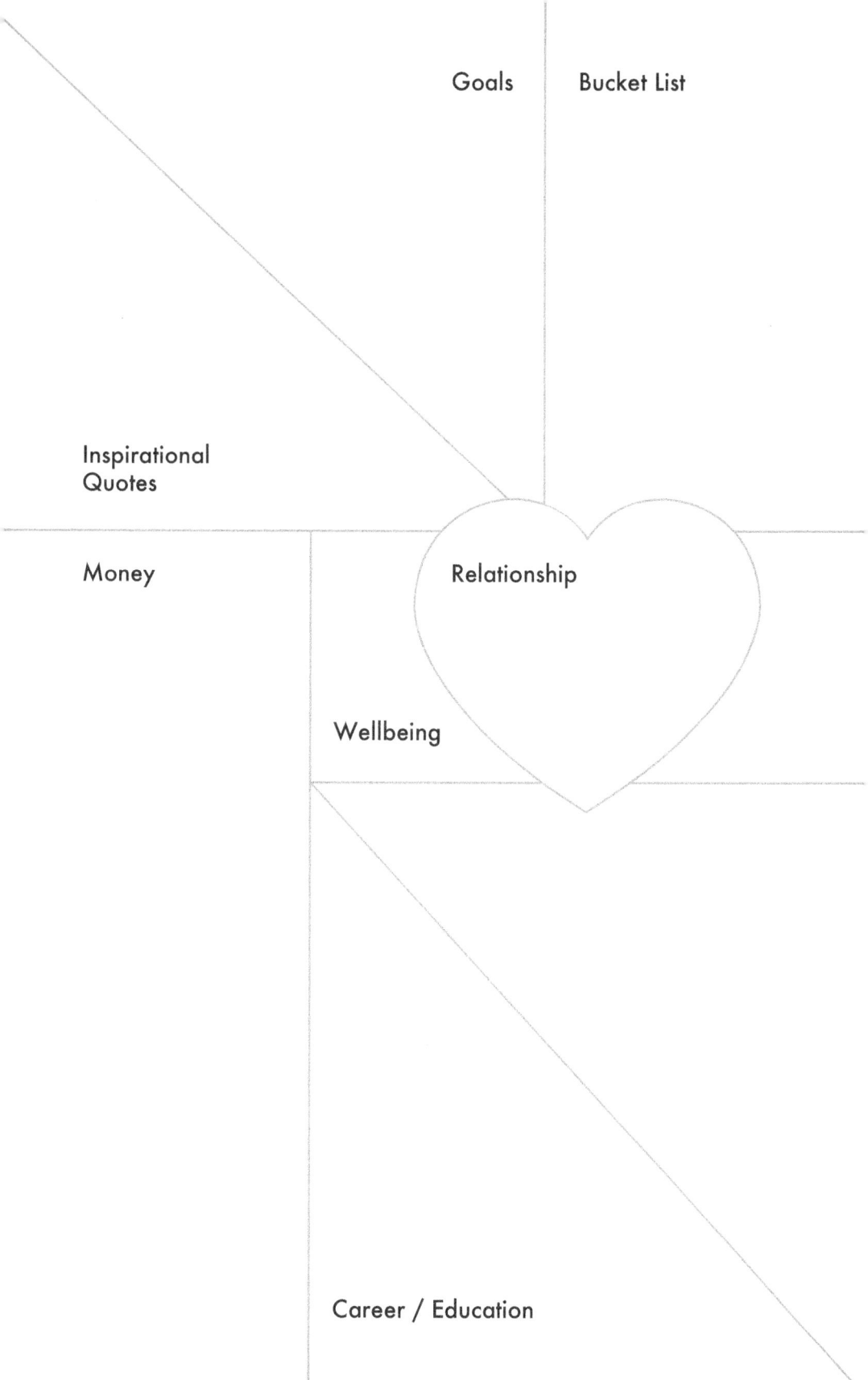

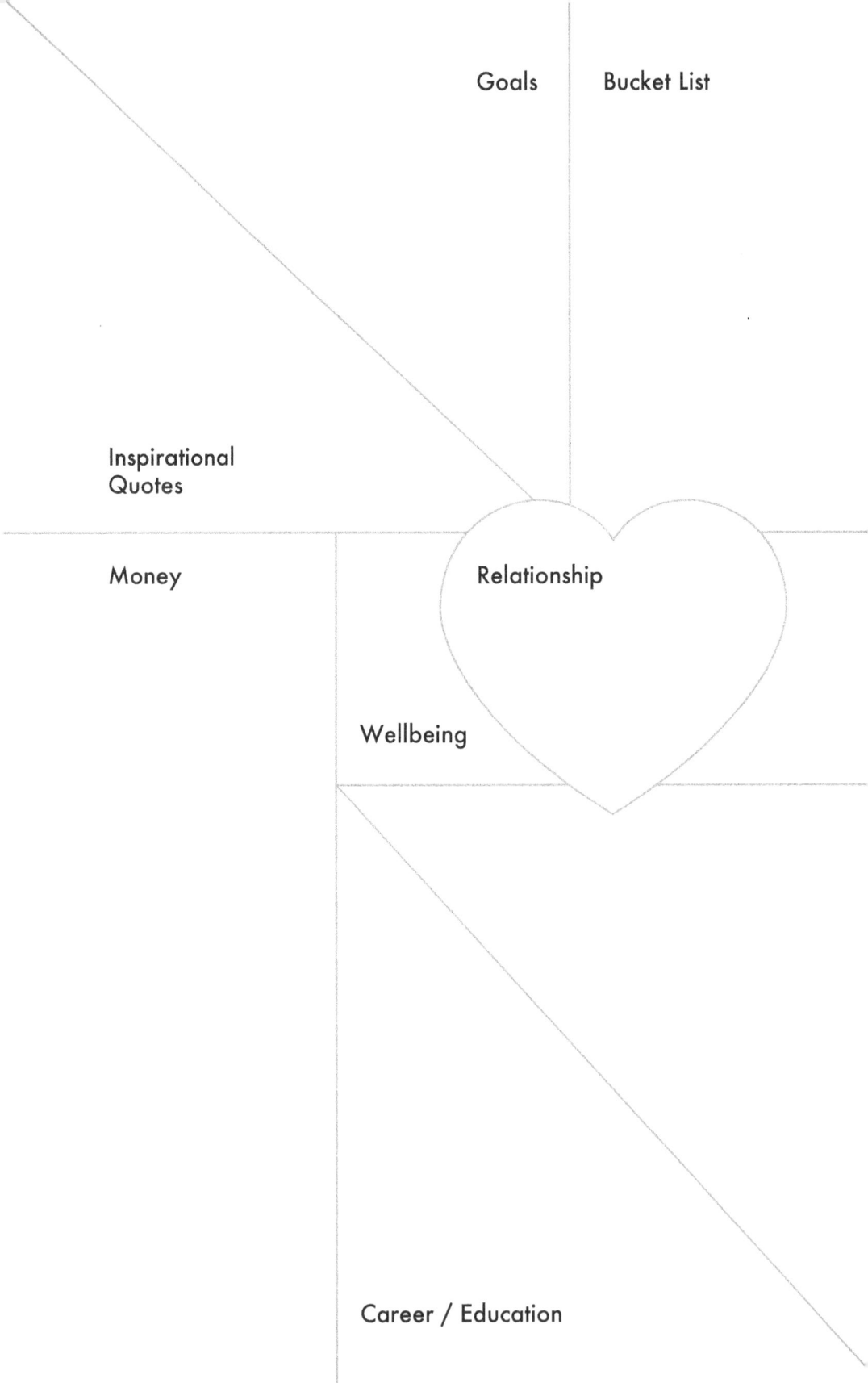

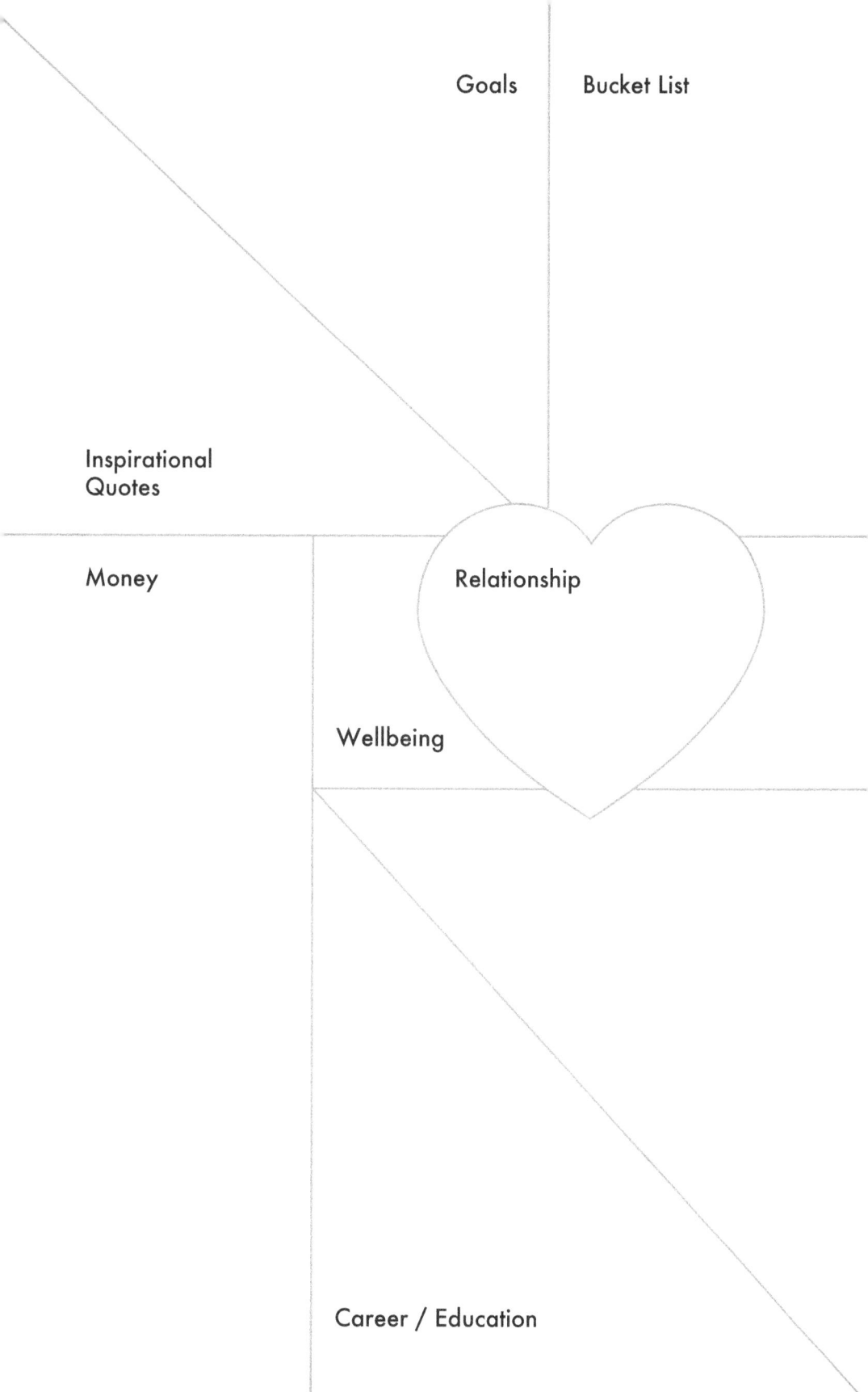

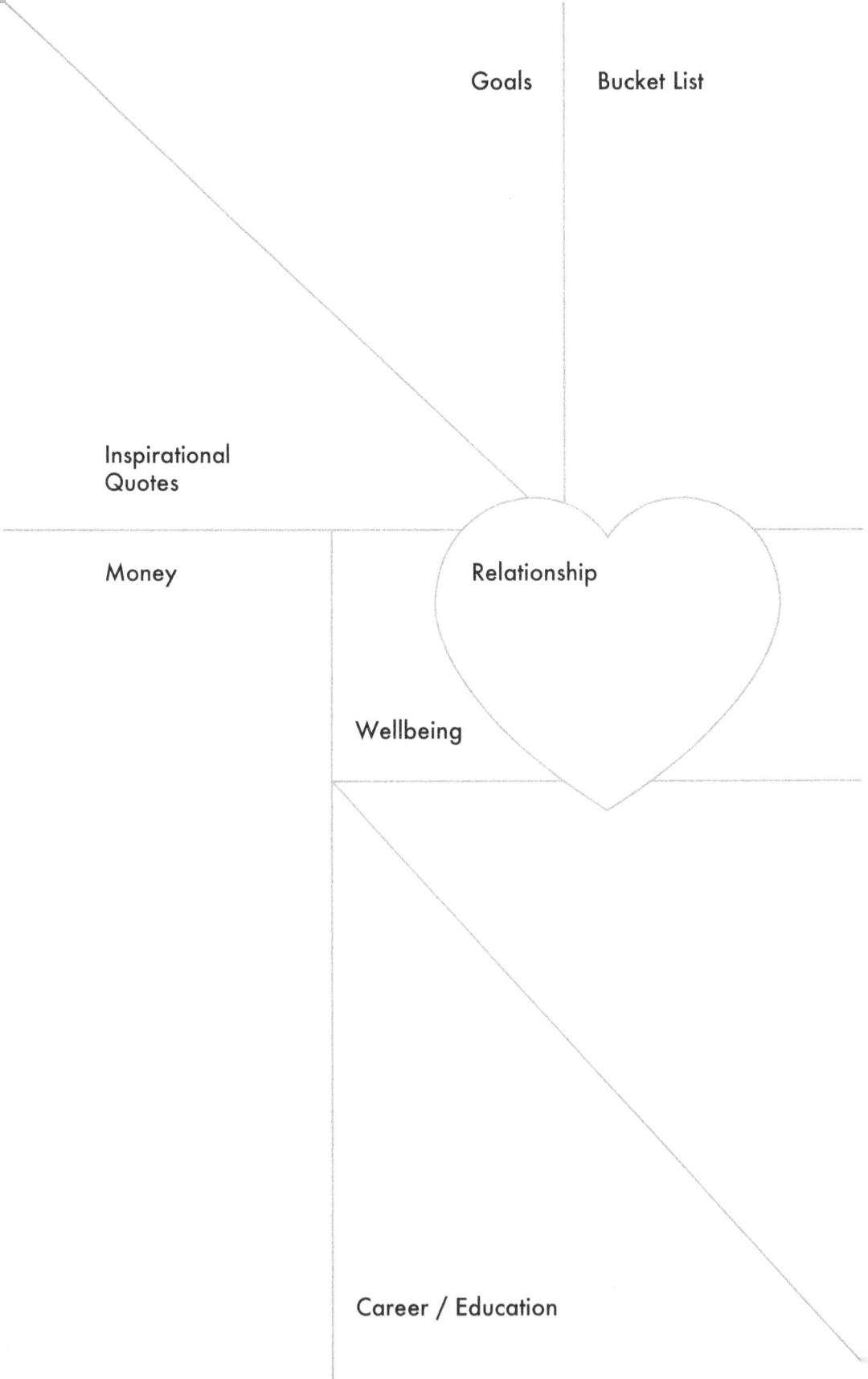

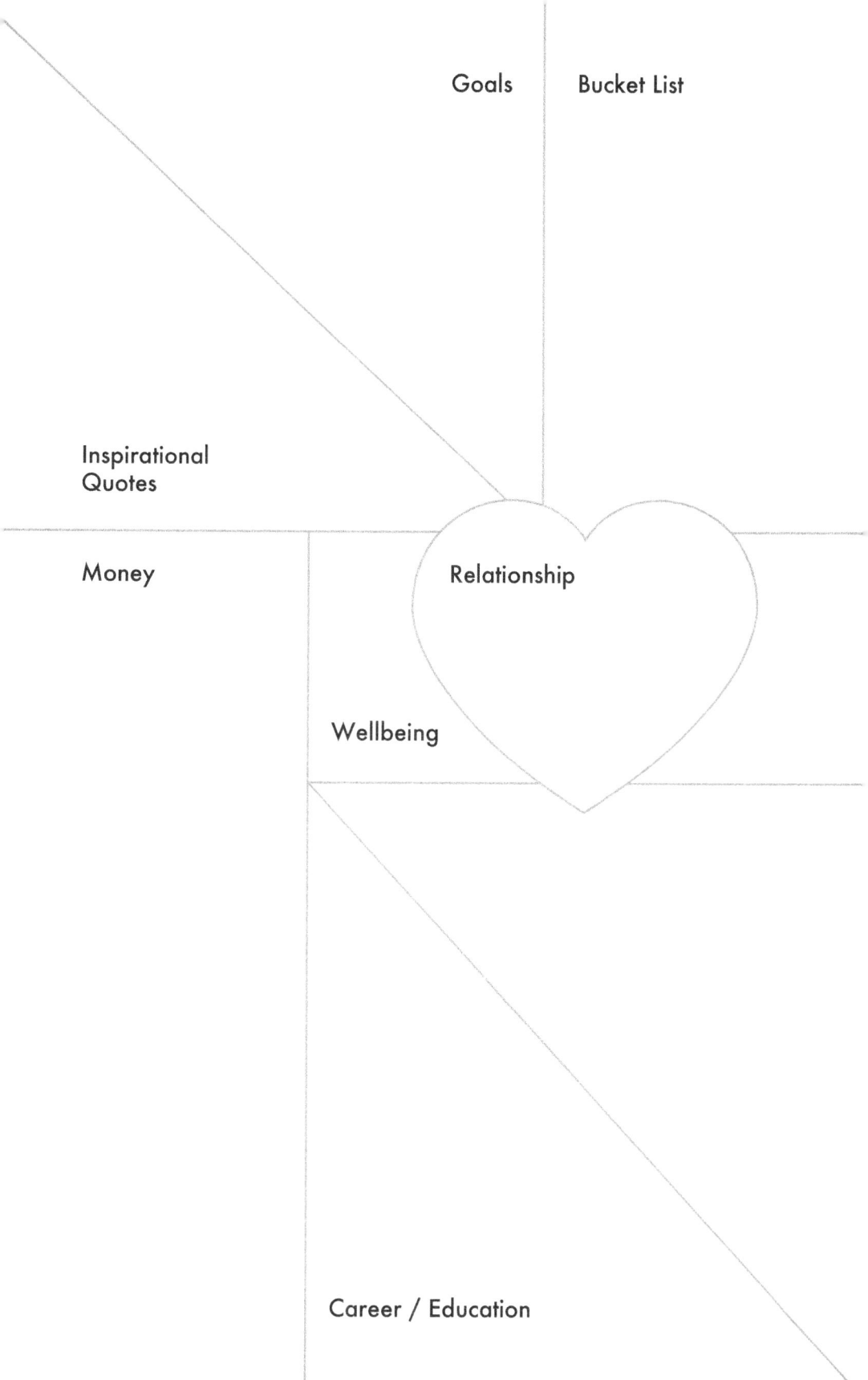

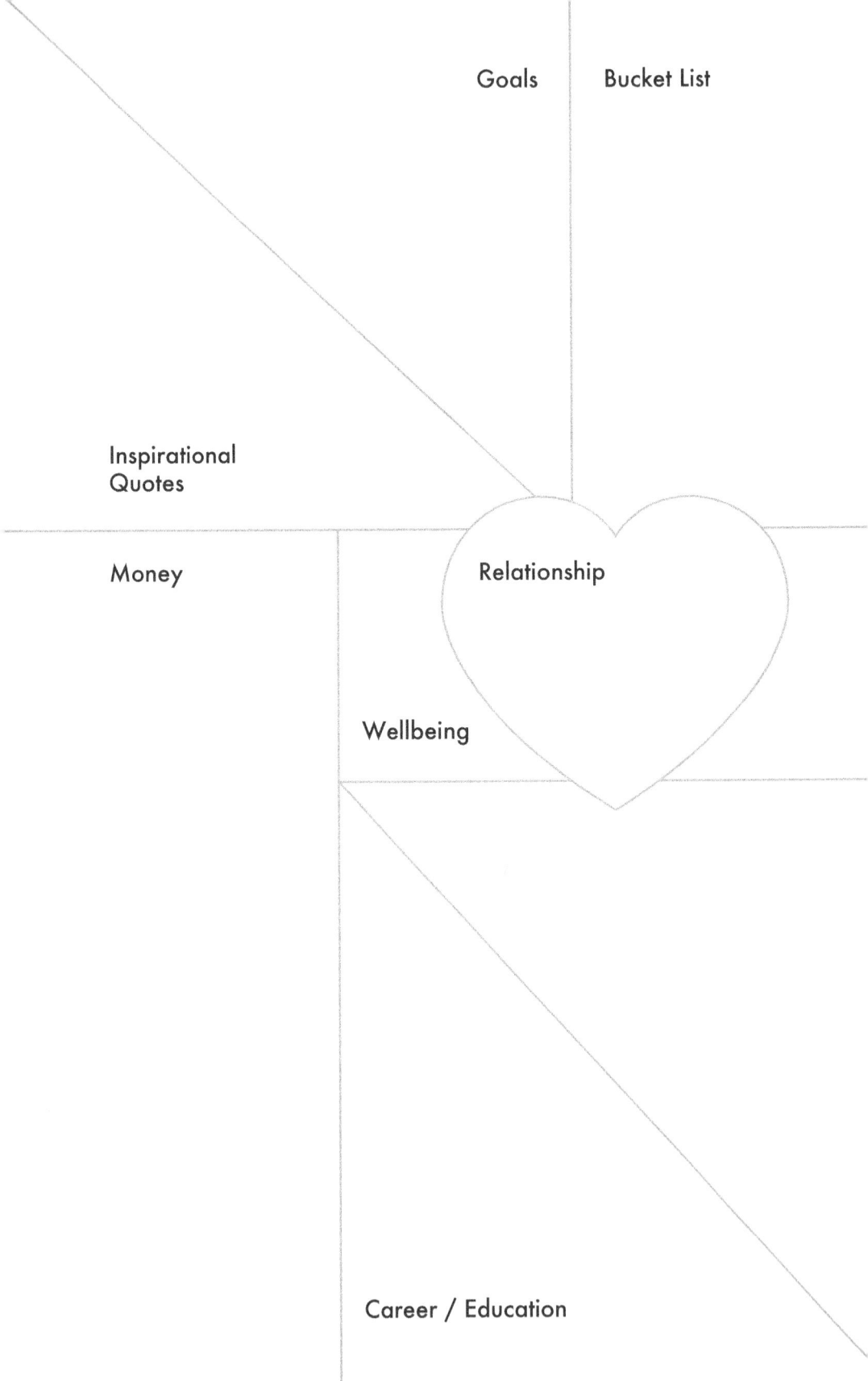

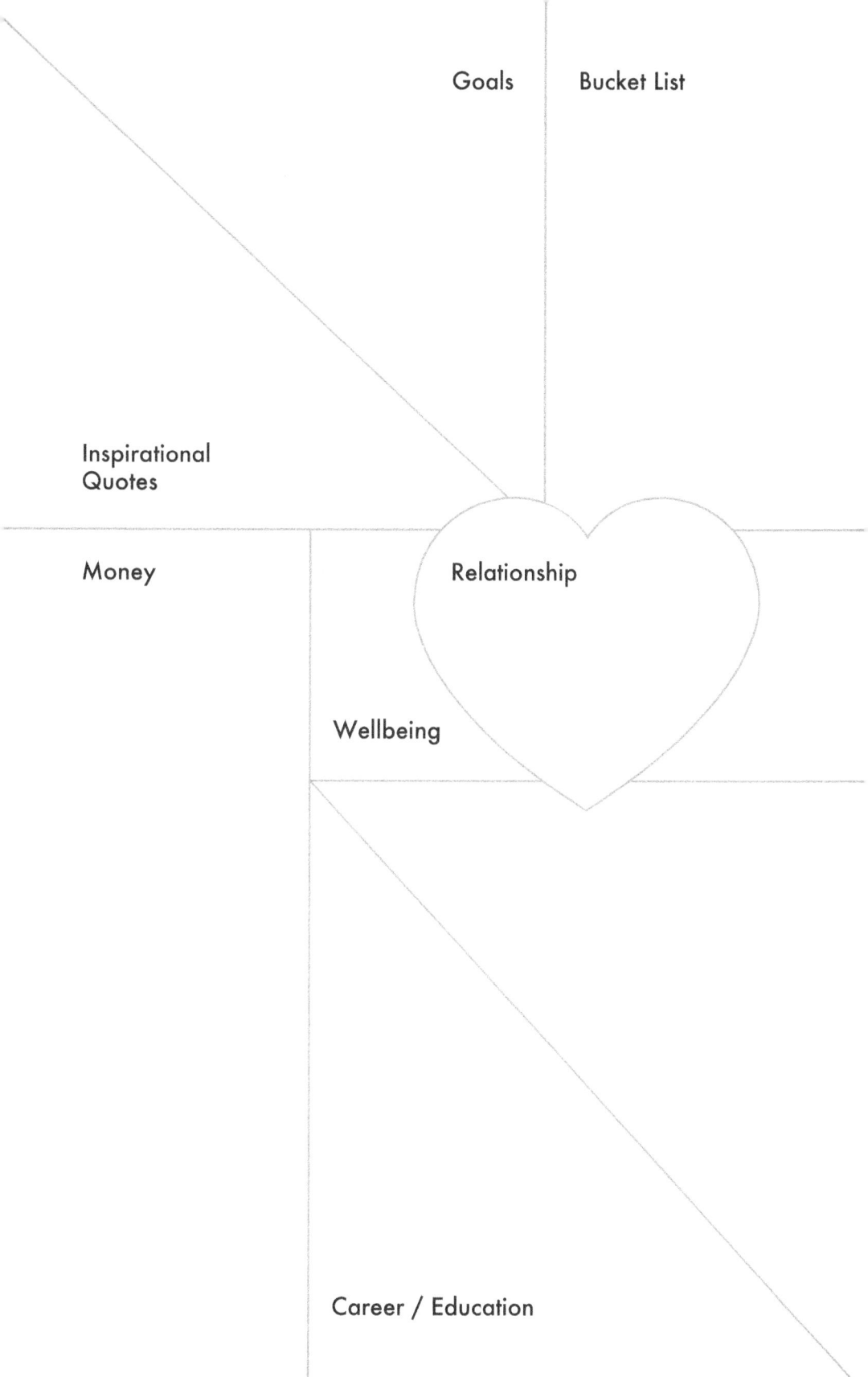

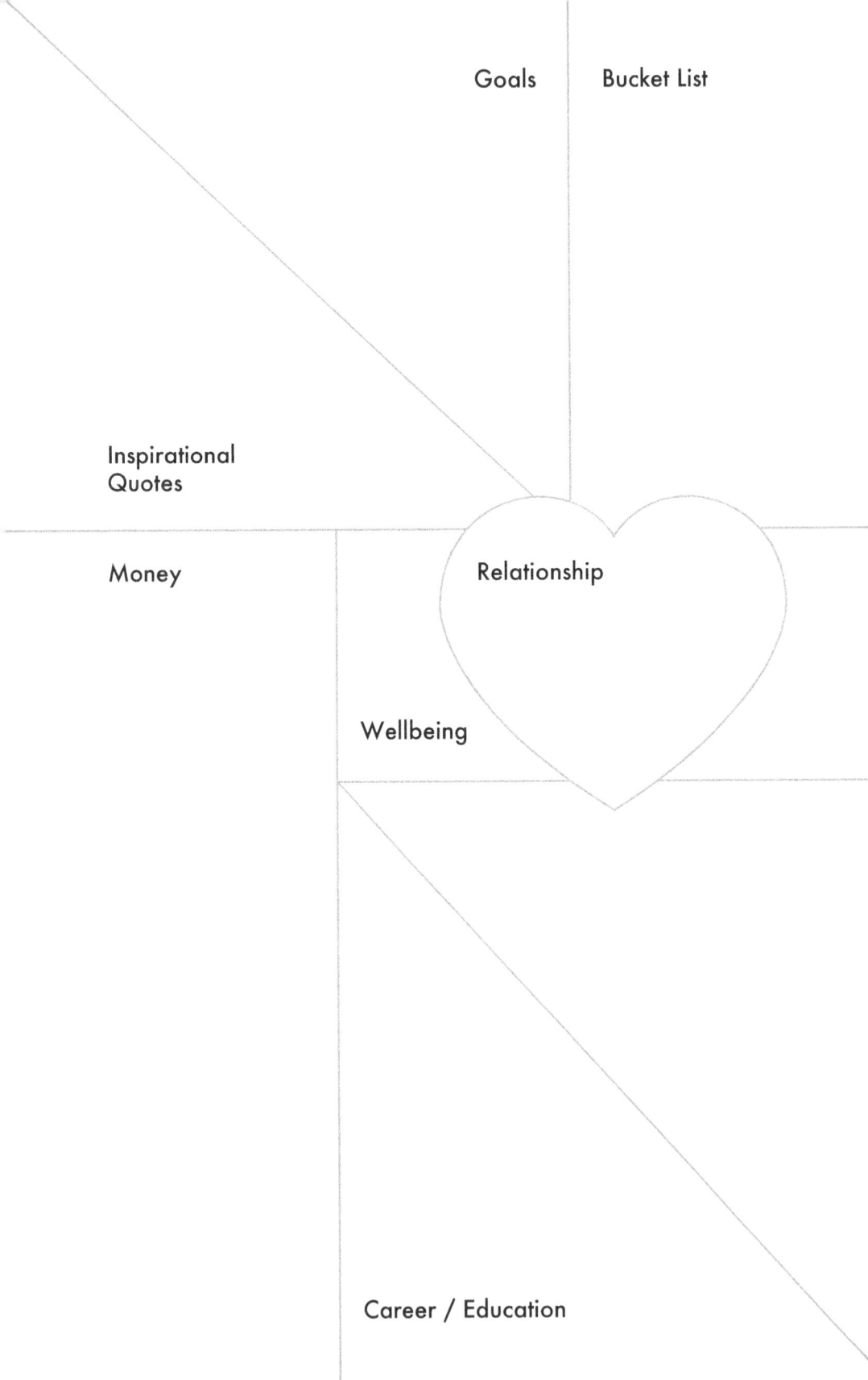

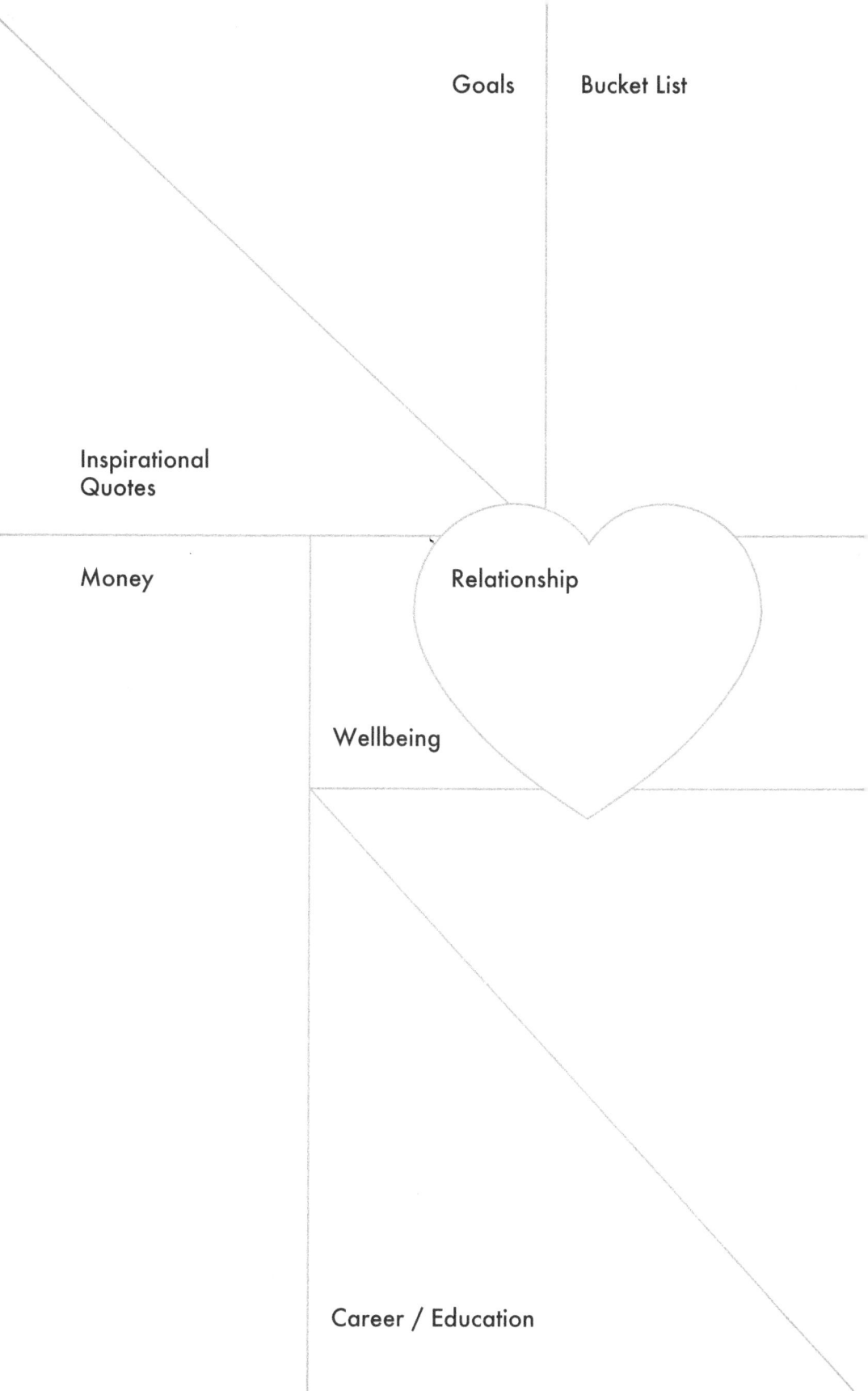

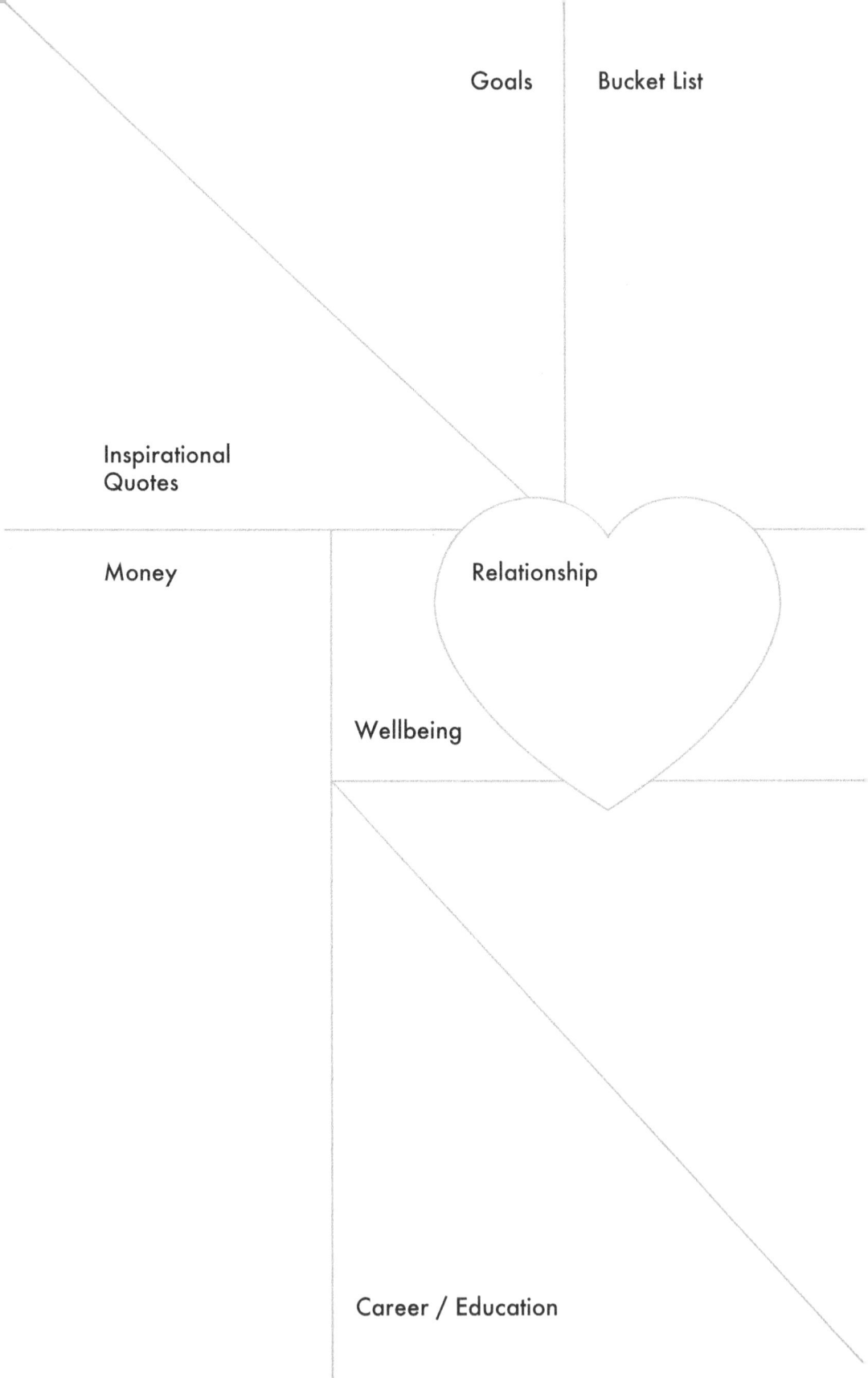

www.ingramcontent.com/pod-product-compliance
Lightning Source LLC
Chambersburg PA
CBHW071408080526
44587CB00017B/3213